AIR RAIDS AND RAF DAYS

1938–1947

S.John Teague
Edited by Helen Allinson and Della Judd

Copyright © 2025: Helen Allinson and Della Judd

All rights reserved. No part of this publication may be produced, distributed, or transmitted in any form or by any means, including photocopying, recording, or other electronic or mechanical methods, without the prior written permission of the publisher, except in the case of brief quotations embodied in critical reviews and certain other non-commercial uses permitted by copyright law.

Photographs—All photographs owned by the Teague family unless otherwise stated.

Published by Synjon Books and Conscious Dreams Publishing
www.synjonbooks.co.uk
www.consciousdreamspublishing.com

Book Consultant: Daniella Blechner

Edited by Helen Allinson, Della Judd, Elise Abram

Typeset by Oksana Kosovan

ISBN: 978-0-904373-26-4

Dedication

For Jack, Louie and Daniel, John's three great grandchildren who gave him so much joy.

Introduction

By Helen Allinson

Father: Sydney

My father, Sydney John Teague (always known as John), was born in 1922 and lived to be 100. His South London childhood was a happy one, but there was very little money as his father was often out of work. This probably added to John's drive and determination to study hard, get qualifications and have a successful career. His Aunt Emm was a vital influence in his life. She was a teacher and, seeing his ability, encouraged and enabled him to take up his scholarship to the grammar school, buying his uniform and the books he needed. It was she who realised how short-sighted he was and got him glasses.

Air Raids and RAF Days

John had to leave school at 16 to pay his way at home, and decided that he would become a librarian. He took an entrance examination to start work at Camberwell Public Libraries.

When war broke out, he was 17 and events catapulted him into adulthood. Straightaway, he was transferred to the air raid control centre in the basement of Camberwell Town Hall and then, in 1940, during the Blitz, given great responsibility in requisitioning empty houses and re-homing bombed-out families.

He volunteered for the R.A.F. hoping to be in the aircrew, but his eyesight wasn't good enough, and he was trained to be a wireless operator mechanic. He served from January 1942 until late 1946, and his postings ranged from Padgate to Lyneham and abroad in Brussels and Holland from 1944. He continued studying for library qualifications whilst in the R.A.F., turning down advancement there.

He stored the diaries that form the main part of this book until he was in his 80s. He then carefully typed them on the computer and threw them away! For his 90th birthday, my brother and I decided to have the text formatted with family photographs and nine copies printed, one for each member of the family. He was pleased with the result but unwilling to have the book printed for the public because of 'libellous remarks' he had made about various officers, although we assured him that they would all have died of old age by then.

And so the book remained until, after his death in 2022, I read the wartime letters from his parents, which he had kept all his life. He had shown us a couple of them a few years before he died, and we had asked if there were many more. He said he had recently disposed of most of them, believing nobody else would find them of interest. Luckily, he kept those included here which, together with the diaries, form a vivid piece of social history that will be of considerable interest to a wider public than his family. The letters record the strain of living with constant bombing raids in a damaged house whilst John's father worked as a full-time air raid warden.

About the editing of book:

His daughter, Helen Allinson painstakingly edited all of the diaries and letters. As much as possible we have left the original text as it was written, with minimal changes. Only where a clarification is needed we have added an extra word or two. These can be seen in square brackets in italics: [*addition*].

John often went back through his diary and made additional notes and sometimes added text when he had been researching in the archives. These can be seen in brackets in italics: (*addition*).

We have made some formatting changes for consistency. For example, monetary values were written in a variety of ways. Where they were written in full we have left those as is, for example, four pence. Otherwise we have used the notation for pounds, shillings and pence. For example, £5 / 3 / 2 to indicate five pounds, three shillings and four pence.

John Teague in his 80s.

For ease of reading we have made grammatical changes and made slight amendments to the sentence structure, adding full stops, for example.

For anyone interested in how ordinary Londoners coped on the home front amidst constant bombing raids or interested in the R.A.F. during the war, this will make a rewarding read.

The Teague family at the time of the diaries

Father: Sydney Teague

John's father was born in 1878 in Peckham and lived his whole life in South London. His father had worked in the leather trade, and Syd was the youngest of the family. He had a variety of jobs, including managing the Bioscope Cinema in Camberwell in his youth, when he enjoyed membership in the Hatcham Liberal Club, New Cross.

Syd became a postman in 1902 and later worked in the leather trade. His life was coloured by the misfortune, as he saw it, of been found unfit to serve in the First World War when he volunteered in 1916 aged 38.

Syd when he was young.

In 1920, when Syd was 40 and Maude Homewood was 27, they were married. Syd was out of work for long periods in the 1930's but still dressed in a smart blue suit, stiff white collar and highly polished boots and went off to 'work' each day so the neighbours would not know he was unemployed. His waistcoat was graced by a gold chain and watch until it had to be pawned, along with his wedding and signet rings. He usually spent the day applying for jobs and walking the streets of the city he knew and loved so well.

He and Maude lived at a number of Brockley addresses, always renting, and finally moving to 21 St Norbert Road in 1938. Finding the money for the weekly rent was often a worry.

21 St Norbert Road, Brockley, where John grew up.

Syd served as a full-time air raid warden during the Second World War, a job he was pleased to undertake but which took a toll on his health.

Baby John with his mother in the garden at St Norbert Rd, Brockley.

Mother: Maude Homewood

Maude Homewood was born in 1893 in Brockley. Her father was a police constable, and her mother a cook. She had three older brothers and was constantly required to help her mother. She herself became a good home cook.

Maude Homewood when she was young.

On leaving school, she worked as an 'ornamental hair worker', according to the 1911 census records. This involved making hairpieces and wigs.

During the First World War, she enrolled as a postwoman, and that was how she and Syd met. They were based at Hatcham Sorting Office. Whilst on duty, she suffered an injured foot caused by shrapnel from a bomb.

Maude in her postwoman's uniform.

Maude had been engaged to a cousin before meeting Syd, but she and Syd enjoyed a happy marriage. Once married, Maude was required to resign from the post office, as was the rule then.

She was a devoted member of the Methodist Church and belonged to the Mother's Meeting there. She and Syd took the children to services in the evening and sent them to Sunday School in the afternoon. She loved poetry and kept a notebook into which she copied her favourites. She had a pleasant singing voice and loved the weekly family occasions at her parents' house when everyone sang old favourites round the piano.

Sister: Ida Teague

Ida was a year older than John and his only sibling.

John and Ida.

Ida.

When Ida left school, she had sufficient style and confidence to obtain work at Selfridges' ladies' clothing department.

She was good-looking and interested in fashion. She knew what she wanted and stood up to her father, which took a bit of doing.

Aunt Emm

Emma Teague, John's aunt, spent her working life as a teacher at the London County Council School, Girls Department, Woods Road, Peckham. She never married and so, as a spinster living with her parents, was able to afford regular holidays abroad.

Emm with her class of girls.

Aunt Emm when she was young.

Aunt Emm was old enough to be John's grandmother, but there was a strong bond between them.

By 1926, Emm was living at Norbury in her newly-built retirement house she bought for £850 freehold, using her lump-sum pension payment.

*Emm's house in Norbury 5,
[later re-numbered 9], Colebrook Road.*

During the 1930s, Ida and John were old enough to stay with Aunt Emm and go away on holiday with her.

Syd was probably Emm's favourite brother, being the youngest, and he certainly needed financial help, so these holidays were a way of helping him without alienating his brothers, for she was always fair to all. In 1931, John stayed at Norbury for a week during the summer holidays, and the next year, both Ida and John stayed, and Auntie took them to many of the museums and places of leisure in the London region.

In 1933, she took them to Herne Bay for a fortnight's holiday, staying full board in a boarding house. This was followed by Bognor Regis in both 1934 and 1935 and Felixstowe in both 1936 and 1937.

Aunt Emm also stayed regularly with friends, the Leslies', at Corby, on the River Eden near Carlisle, and that was where she died, aged 75, during the war, having been bombed out of her home.

Grandad Homewood: John Homewood

John Homewood was born in 1860 and served as a London police constable from 1882 to 1907, rejoining during the First War. He had the misfortune of losing the sight of one eye in the course of his duties. He was attempting to arrest a burglar, who jumped from a garden wall and hit him in the eye with a jemmy (crowbar).

After retirement, at the end of the First World War, John became a uniformed civil servant at Somerset House. His job was to get out volumes of birth, marriage and death indexes for the public from the great warren of basement rooms, carrying the heavy volumes up and down many flights of stairs.

Grandad Homewood.

He was over six foot, upright in bearing, easy going and charming

When he died in 1954, he was the oldest police pensioner in London.

1938

Over to John's words now.

My habit of keeping a detailed diary appears to have originated in June 1938, when I was 16. It was at first in part scribbled in pencil and part written in ink in a fragmentary hard-bound account book.

June

General Schools Examination, 16 June to 5 July, oral exams in French and Spanish.

Brockley Grammar School, postcard.

July

End of term, 26 July my last day at [*Brockley Grammer School for Boys*]. I have submitted two poems and an essay to Mr Lee for possible publication in *The Raven*. [*John's parents could not afford for him to stay on at school, and it was now vital that he earned money as his father was out of work again.*]

I have received a testimonial from Dr Sinclair [*the headmaster*] and have already written to Camberwell Borough Council to sit their examination for junior clerks which is necessary for a job in the public library. I have been helping in the school library. [*Years later, John noted that in those days the public library service was an important cultural and leisure provision of local authorities. Librarians had some status in the community.*]

August

I went on holiday to Wells in Somerset with Auntie Emm. One of my best holidays. We visited Glastonbury, Wookey Hole, Cheddar and Burnham-on-Sea.

14 September

I went to Stillness Road Evening Institute [*Camberwell*] and was advised to do a general preliminary professional course in preparation for any entrance exam that might come along.

20 September

I joined the Old Boys' Association. I was allowed to use Deptford Reference Library for the first time [*lending library only up till then*]. One of my poems is in *The Raven*. My friend Caswallon Evans said he thought it was good.

21 September

Dad went to Mrs Seager's funeral, she was 93, an old friend of Dad and Emm and their parents. [*Catherine Seager lived in Ivydale Road, Nunhead*].

23 September

I sat for Camberwell Borough entrance exam at the South East London Art Gallery, Peckham Road, 09:00–12:00 and 13:00–17:00. Questions were hard. There were about 200 entrants. Hitchcock and Blackman were there, Blackman is still at school, but Hitchcock had left, he is about 19, no job yet.

[*John refers to boys he has been at school with by their surnames as that is how they were addressed at school, apart from close friends, such as Doug Latham.*]

24 September

I sat for the remainder of the Camberwell exam. Blackman told me that arrangements have been made to evacuate all schoolchildren from London in the event of war. Each has to keep a case containing pyjamas, toothbrush etc. at school. A warning will be given over the wireless and children, if at home, will have to go to school and leave for camps in the country.

26 September

I started at evening classes, Stillness Road. Met White at the tram stop, he has got a job in a bank. He has one glass eye. Standing, who has got work at the Electricity Offices in Lewisham, joined my class. Met Shearing on way home, his father in the Navy (he has a young father). He says that Hilly Fields and the school are closed and occupied by the Army and they have a gun mounted on the flat part of the school roof. There was a speech by Hitler, vague and full of insults to Czechoslovakia. If there is a war it will begin next Saturday, I expect. Yesterday Mantle Road School was open for fitting gas masks, we did not go.

John at this time.

28 September

Met Doug Latham who has stayed on at school, he confirms that it is now closed and that he is to go to a camp in the country. He does not want to leave his mother behind, but arrangements have been made for his young brother to go with him. [*The 1939 Register shows that Doug and his brother were evacuated to Wadhurst.*]

I tied up some of my books in bundles so that they can be moved if an incendiary bomb hits my bedroom. In the evening Mum, Dad, Ida and I went to be fitted with respirators. Schoolchildren have not yet left London.

I went to evening classes and later searchlights were practising overhead. Roosevelt sent a second telegram to Hitler in reply to Hitler's reply to his last one. He suggested a European Conference of all directly concerned in the Czechoslovak/German question, at some neutral place. Chamberlain has already recalled Parliament and told the truth about all his visits to Hitler and had begged for a meeting between Hitler and the British and French Prime Ministers. Chamberlain told Parliament that he was quite sure that a settlement could be reached within one week and Hitler had agreed to such a meeting. It is to take place tomorrow, Thursday, in Germany.

All territorials have been called up. Today all Navy reservists were recalled and a start was made on digging trenches in all available open spaces in British towns as air raid cover and several Tube stations were closed for 'structural alterations'. Now Hitler has agreed to meet the ministers of other countries in a last attempt to get his way without war.

29 September

Mussolini, Hitler, Daladier and Chamberlain met at Munich, with Mussolini as mediator! By 01:30 Friday morning agreement was reached. Czechoslovakia is to be partially dismembered, but peace has been kept, at least for the time being! I went to evening classes.

30 September

Russia said of the Four-Power Committee that it is a committee for the coordination of Fascist aggression.

1 October

A letter and stamps from Auntie Emm. She is pleased with my poem in *The Raven*. She is very much afraid that war will come.

Sunday, 2 October

Went to Sunday School in afternoon with Doug Latham and then [*Methodist*] church in the evening with Doug and our whole family. Prayers for peace were said. Doug and I went forward and signed the students' roll: 'To promise to serve Christ only.' Doug's father is a non-believer and his mother is Church of England but we were carried by the Rev. Arnold Bellwood's enthusiasm. He is a violent and enthusiastic pacifist preacher; a Socialist, I am certain. Dad misses Rev. Bamford's gentlemanly preaching.

20 October [*the next entry*]

Purchased an Old Brockleians tie, very nice. It is black with brown, gold and green stripes with ravens in between. I telephoned Camberwell re employment. I am promised notification in about a fortnight. There will be only six jobs, but my name is first on the list.

Sunday, 23 October

Went with Mum and Dad to Auntie's and had a very good day.

24 October

Went to Peckham with Dad to buy him a lighter at the Co-op, Mum's birthday present to him, 8/6d. I bought him a tie press and two Penguin books. I shall use the tie press as well, for the Old Boys' tie. I went to the Central Library in afternoon and classes in the evening.

25 October

Received Mrs Leighton's old wireless set and spent morning fitting it up, changing the terminals etc. It will be better than the one in my room. Library afternoon, classes in evening. Thick fog.

26 October

Mr Blanchard, our lodger, was taken ill. Mum went up to tell his people and the doctor sent for. Acute bronchitis. I had to give up my key to them for the time being.

27 October

Mr B. dressed and went to the lavatory [*outside*], went back in and had a heart attack. All telephones were in use and some delay in getting through to Dr Nelson and Mr B. died whilst the doctor was with him. [*William Blanchard was 74.*] His son [*Colin*] was mayor of Deptford and they lived in a council house farther up our road.

I began to despair of ever hearing from Camberwell and made increased numbers of applications for jobs advertised in *The Daily Telegraph* and *The Times*, which I scanned daily at the Public Library (20 minutes' walk each way).

Dad came with me to Rye Lane, where at the 35/- Tailors, I bought a blue business suit.

November

I applied for positions as junior clerk to Woolwich Polytechnic, and Paddington Borough Council among others, and had interviews at London Hospital, Thomas Cook and Son, Drapers' and General Insurance Co., London and Provincial Insurance Co. and Southern Railway. Several of these offered me employment at £1 a week when the going rate was 25/-.

I turned them down and, in any case, I tended to tell them that I had passed top in the entrance examination for Camberwell Public Libraries and was awaiting a vacancy. A strange one was Langley London Limited, Borough High Street, where they wanted assurance that I was a total abstainer and attended church regularly, then asked, 'Which denomination?' All of which seemed irrelevant to being a clerk and I turned down 22/6d a week.

I went home and prayed hard for a post in Camberwell Libraries, feeling guilty at not accepting paid employment when offered whilst we needed the money rather badly.

I had also persuaded my parents not to let the front room anymore, so we were additionally hard up.

The evening classes that I was attending were bookkeeping, which all seemed rather obvious stuff, and Pitman's Shorthand which didn't. The shorthand effort was encouraged by Uncle John who was good at it, having been an early example of a company secretary, though poorly paid. He gave me his notebooks. [*Uncle John Teague and his wife and Aunt Kate lived at 9, Whitford Gardens, Mitcham.*]

On Wednesday was Camberwell Council meeting. God be gracious!

December

I fixed up coloured electric lights at Christmas as usual and blew the main fuse, a very useful experience I expect. It was very cold and snowy. The Elvidges' our Methodist friends sent me a pullover for Christmas and for Mother an enormous family pork pie. They now live at 101, Rasen Lane, Lincoln. They had been servants to the Reverend Bamford and had come to Brockley with him, going back when he retired.

I learned to play Newmarket with a school friend and played it for hours on end for pennies with all and sundry.

I've been reading Agatha Christie *Appointment with Death*, Sydney Horler, *Danger's Bright Eyes* and Edgar Wallace, *Traitors Gate*.

I cooked a meal on my own for all the family: eggs, bacon, fried tomato and fried bread.

Sunday afternoons were made enjoyable by the afternoon worship for youngsters which had evolved under the new, young, pacifist minister, Rev. Arnold Bellwood, into a debating society. I led several of these debates: 'That the modern world has mistaken comfort for civilisation' and 'That Sunday amusements should be abolished', 'Capital punishment: an obscenity', 'Why does a God of love allow pain and suffering?' and 'Is War inevitable?'.

There was of course much discussion and indoctrination in the pacifist interest, but in the event we all volunteered for the armed services in turn! We usually went to church in the evening as well.

One Sunday I only put 3d in the collection and bought Mum 3d of sweets in Sturmey's with the rest, she was rather unwell or I would have eaten them myself.

Our Wesleyan Church funds were raised by regular bazaars for which most members made and prepared things at home and they were very busy events with the general public crowding in; the one in December 1938 taking as much as £161. Church also ran a Wednesday social evening for young people and I played lots of table tennis.

Apart from visiting Auntie Emm at 5, Colebrook Road, I also visited a friend of hers, an ex-supply teacher of French, Miss Couratin at Playfield Crescent Dulwich. She was French and supplied me with lots of foreign stamps for my collection.

Another ex-teacher friend of Auntie's was Agnes Samuels and I first visited her with Auntie at Foyle Road Blackheath, but later, they bought 308, Baring Road, Lee and their son and family took over the Foyle Road house. She must have been very nice, always inviting Ida and me to her Christmas party, but I was embarrassed by such events, hating party games. Her husband was a sea captain and in retirement he worked as a river pilot, bringing ships up the Thames to London docks.

1939

January

I applied for posts with Castrol Oil, the gas company, London Electric Lighting Company, Bankside, *John Bull* magazine, Southern Railway Hotels and Trix Model Electric Trains. The postage on these letters was three halfpence and Aunt Emm sent me a shilling's worth of stamps.

I got as far as a medical at the gas company and failed on my eyesight, so I wrote to my former headmaster asking him to try to get me a free appointment at Sydenham Children's Hospital as I had only just left school. He did so stretching a point, knowing our circumstances, and I had my eyes tested there the following Thursday. Meanwhile, however, I had landed the job at Trix Trains of Clerkenwell Road, EC2 at 22/6d a week working out in my head costings and invoices for so many gross of tiny parts at odd halfpennies and three halfpennies each.

I was very quick and totally accurate at this and they were very pleased with me, letting me have the Thursday afternoon off to go to the hospital, although it was only my first week. Unfortunately, from that evening Dad had to put belladonna ointment into my eyes at frequent intervals (he was more gentle-handed than Mother), thus making it only just possible to travel to work and impossible to see to work.

This problem was solved by another junior being allocated to reading out the calculations and writing down my solutions!

The next day I had to tell the boss that I had the job I wanted (at Dulwich Library) and would complete only my first week with Trix.

My poor father had forbidden me to utter the phrase that my conscience told me I should, to the effect that I would not expect the full wage of 22/6d. War was imminent. The two bosses, being expatriate German Jews, kept a low profile and sent me the full wages by registered post the following week, having told me earlier, quite correctly, that I was not entitled to a penny. Of course I wrote thanking them.

March

I was required to take air raid precautions courses in council time at Grove Vale Depot. These comprised first aid and gas drill. Working wearing a gas mask was most unpleasant for anyone who wore spectacles for one had first to apply a grease to one's glasses and to the inside of the eyepieces of the gas mask before putting the mask on in order to avoid the thing steaming up with condensation from breathing. Otherwise it proved impossible to see. One had to wear spectacles that fitted closely to the eyes and were secured round the ears.

Instructions from a 1940s cigarette card 'Air raid precautions' printed by W.D. & H.D. Wills

Air Raids and RAF Days

Gas chambers were filled with tear gas for these tests and the gas clung to the clothing and caused the eyes to stream with tears when one came out.

First aid was always a nightmare to me, for when any injury was graphically described, I carried that injury in my mind's eye and felt sick and ill, but, although I must have turned green round the gills on occasion, I never actually fainted. Strangely enough I never even considered how I would cope with a gory war situation.

Other war training proved less troublesome to me. I could cope very well with air raid report centre procedures. We practised receiving telephone messages about imaginary incendiary bomb incidents and gained some experience in speedily dealing with them. We had printed pads on which we recorded the necessary details of address bombed, number of casualties, if known, number of people trapped under the wreckage, if known, and the services needed, such as ambulances, fire engines, rescue squads and bomb disposal units to deal with unexploded bombs.

13 March

I was issued with a gas mask and informed that we were the mainstay of Camberwell's civil defence until a force of volunteers and full-time people were trained and in place. What with work on split duties and this training I needed a weekend away at Auntie Emm's. She took me to lunch at Slater's in the Strand, to the British Museum and National Gallery as well as to Kew. Back at work on the Monday.

Other Saturdays when I was not working, I went on rambles with Doug Latham as per the *Geographia* Kent and Surrey ramblers' books. Doug and I also messed about with old radio sets bought for the odd bob or two in junk shops in Deptford. We made them work and each had one in our bedrooms.

26 April

A man dropped dead in Reading Room. I began to see life!

12 May

Mr Joyce assaulted Weatherall in the Lending Department. I was standing next to him at the counter and dialled 999 as the blood poured from his nose and the glass from his spectacles spread over the issue tickets. The police arrived within 10 minutes and the victim decided not to prosecute. [*Weatherall was a pacifist, and William Joyce later evolved into the traitor 'Lord Haw-Haw', and broadcast sedition from Nazi Germany.*]

24 May

Grandmother Homewood's funeral at Brockley Cemetery. Mother went, but the rest of us did not. That was a family row that did not heal. (*Grandmother had loaned Maude money now and then to tide the family through the week. But one day she demanded it back much sooner than agreed. There was a row in front of John and Ida when they were children and then all contact was cut off for some years.*)

Mary Homewood (nee Tulloch) died, aged 76, and was buried in Brockley Cemetery.

Sunday, 28 May

My birthday. A lovely day. I led a family group on a ramble to Eynsford. Mum, Dad, Ida and Ida's boyfriend, Len, all came and I tired them out. The fare was 2/3d each.

4 June

I had my shoes re-heeled which cost 1/8d and the cleaning and re-proofing of my raincoat cost 3/-.

2 July

My very kind aunt once again took me on holiday. We went to Bognor, where I had already stayed at Aldwick with her friends, the Noakes. He is a World War One gas victim, running a modern house by taking in summer visitors on full board. That evening we all went to a Moral Rearmament meeting (my aunt's current interest).

The holiday included coach trips to Petworth, Midhurst and Slindon. It was a very windy week. I spent 14/1d of my savings on presents, postcards and stamps, including 9d towards the cost of the vet for my cat Billy. Ida did not come, having grown out of these holidays.

Aunt Emm at Bognor.

August

I was considered reliable enough to be sent down to the Livesey Branch Library in the Old Kent Road to be in charge for an evening duty.

Uncle Jack [*Homewood*] and Aunt Vi paid a very rare visit, they live at Mottingham.

War Comes

All over the country, local government had the biggest task in its history. Hundreds of thousands of people were evacuated from danger zones. Town halls, public baths and other buildings were protected, trenches were dug and taxis and private cars were requisitioned as fire tenders.

1 September

German planes raiding Poland. I was ordered to put myself at the full-time disposal of the air raid control officer at Camberwell Town Hall.

The shifts were 23:00–07:00, 07:00–15:00 and 15:00–23:00. Of course there was no sleep on night shifts and when I was at home I was disturbed by all-night bombing.

3 September

We were at war from 11:00, with air raid alerts from 11:00–11:30, 02:00 and 03:00–03:30.

September

We made numerous cups of tea to make life tolerable, paying eight pence each a week. Innumerable games of chess were another time-passer. These shifts put paid to my attendance at church activities other than the occasional attendance on Sunday evening, usually just Mother and me.

Camberwell Public Libraries, in common with others, were still operating but with restricted hours and skeleton staff and I visited now and again to see my colleagues and to borrow books to augment the very good Deptford Central Library of my own borough.

Deptford Library (courtesy of Southwark Archives).

Sometimes I would walk to Dulwich when I was off during the day being on night shift, and play table tennis with Nobby Clarke, the caretaker, and the air raid wardens housed in the basement there.

6 October

Ida stayed out all night. A very startling fact. Dad walked round to the police station and they checked on her known friends. He waited and at 02:30, he was informed that she was at a Hampstead address (which was among those he had given). It was that of a work colleague of hers at Selfridges.

As my shift on the Saturday did not begin until 23:00, I telephoned Selfridges that morning and they reluctantly brought Ida to the phone and I stressed to her that she must come home after work and talk to Father. She arrived after 19:00 trailing along an insipid-looking Canadian, not a serviceman but a civilian. Dad was furious and Mum and I had to restrain him from assaulting this character.

Eventually, after a meal, they were allowed out for the evening with Ida to be in by 22:30. I went round to the Maypole Off Licence and bought Dad a quart bottle of ale, then I went off to work.

14 October

The sinking of the *Royal Oak* in Scapa Flow Harbour, by torpedoes with the loss of 800 lives.

Grandad Homewood comes to dinner on Sundays since Grandmother died. We walk him back to Endwell Road at teatime.

16 October

There were air raids on the Firth of Forth, missing the bridge but hitting a battleship. The next day the *Iron Duke* was hit in Scapa Flow in an air raid.

The kitten I gave to Doug Latham is thriving.

There are shortages of bacon and meat in the shops. I bought an attaché case in Rye Lane, British Home Stores for 1/11d and replaced the brown paper blackout on my bedroom window with boarding.

Doug Latham.

November

Sometimes I went to see Aunt Emm in the day and went on to work by tram from Norbury for the 23:00 start.

We paid a visit to Mother's relations, the Flemings, in Brixton.

December

By mid-month the council had managed to set up a canteen that operated for lunch and tea only (although the councillors and senior Town Hall staff were served breakfast there). This was on the top floor and tea was a penny a cup, coffee two pence and egg-on-chips, which became my staple diet, four pence.

John wearing Royal Air Force Reserve badge.

23 December

I visited Rye Lane Peckham and bought puff pastry at Kennedy's (with which Mother made mince-pies, she had already made the mincemeat in November), handkerchiefs and cigars for Dad for four shillings, chocolates for Ida at four shillings, a teapot for Mother at three shillings and sixpence-halfpenny plus a tin-opener at sixpence.

By Christmas I was well set into the routine of shift work at the Air Raid Report Centre in the basement of Camberwell Town Hall. The building was completed in 1934 and was just an ordinary building with the basement strengthened with timber struts and beams, it would not have withstood a direct bomb hit nor would the basement have held the weight of the collapsed building for more than a minute or two and yet it was the wartime control point for a whole London borough of some quarter of a million people. [*It still stands and is now known as Southwark Town Hall.*]

*Camberwell Town Hall
(1920's Guide to the Borough of Camberwell)*

Christmas Day

I was on duty from 07:00 until 15:00 when I walked home. Grandad Homewood spent the day with us and we had our Christmas dinner at 16:30 and I stayed up late. We enjoyed ourselves! [*Grandad John Homewood was 79 at this time.*]

After Christmas

Doug Latham and I very often spent time together at our house or his, playing chess, visiting Deptford Public Library together, etc. and we each gave the other a 'party' around Christmastime. He lived two minutes walk away at 54, Arica Road.

I was reading J.B. Priestley's *Good Companions*, then his plays *I Have Been Here Before* and *Time and the Conways*, having started a collection of all his books. Douglas Reed's *Insanity Fair*, on the world situation impressed me.

Ordinary social life went on as much as possible and, I would occasionally take Mother to the cinema; one such trip was to Lewisham Gaumont to see *Five Came Back*, another *Les Misérables* and *Thirty-nine Steps* (in one programme!), and, of course, *Goodbye Mr. Chips*. I would pay for her seat and she would pay the bus or tram fare and buy the choc ices. Dad disdained cinema under the general dismissive 'rubbish' though he enjoyed theatre.

Lewisham Gaumont Palace Cinema, (courtesy of Southwark Archives).

1940

1 January

I have taken ten shillings out of my Post Office Savings towards the 10/6d fee for the Library Association, to be paid back as soon as possible. Balance £1/10/9 but I owe Dad 9/-. Work 17:00–23:00.

2 January

We have at last succeeded, after deputations, in getting breakfast for us six library folk after night duty and we are to be allowed to sleep when all's quiet (as the councillors and senior Town Hall staff do), but no beds for us. We are also to get time off for Christmas duty and four months of overtime, but no overtime pay. I am owed 14 hours per week over four months of overtime. Mr Cobley told me that he could not see how I could ever get back anything like that, AS THERE WAS A WAR ON. On duty from 17:00–23:00.

Staff at the air raid report centre. John on right beside Lily Mocklin.

3 January

First whole day off. Wired electric light into Mother's pantry. Repaired old wireless.

5 January

They have set up a canteen especially for our Air Raid Control Centre, cheap and perhaps the result of the fuss we six library staff have made? Evening to see Doug, played chess. He has left school but has no job as yet. He has improved his mother's kitchen. They own the house in Arica Rd.

Sunday, 6 January

On duty 9:00–17:00. I have caught Doug's cold. He is going after a job at Brixton, here's luck to him. I joined the Association of Assistant Librarians.

7 January

Worked 09:00–17:00. In evening took down Christmas decorations a day early, I hope that that will not prove to be unlucky. Met Doug delivering newspapers this morning, he was a little embarrassed.

8 January

I paid for Library Association correspondence course from Mr Martin. Evening played chess with Doug.

10 January

On 09:00–17:00. Air raid YELLOW ALERT, from 11:19 to 11:50. Finished reading *I Worked in a Soviet Factory* by F. Francis. Good and informative.

11 January

On night shift so free during day and went to see Mr Gilman, librarian at Dulwich. He said that he was outraged to have lost me to the control centre and perhaps I should go sick. I said that I could not do that unless I was sick and he said that I looked very tired, which I was. On 23:00–09:00 with YELLOW warning but also two hours sleep and breakfast at 06:00. I taught Miss Harding (Civil Defence staff) my duties, so that I could take charge (until someone senior arrived) if there was a raid and I was the only council officer there at the time.

12 January

On night shift, 23:00–09:00. YELLOW. We also had an action exercise, a great surprise and the first of its kind. We sent out rescue parties, police, fire brigade etc. in operational gear. Only a few mistakes made such as a light rescue party not going out when we told them, thinking it only another paper exercise. They were reprimanded.

Saturday, 13 January

Home 09:55 bed until 17:30 but could sleep only three hours. On again 23:00.

14 January

Some sleep on duty plus breakfast 06:00 bacon, eggs, toast, marmalade and tea.

Monday, 15 January

Off 09:00 back on again 23:00. Only 10 of us turned up. Most of the volunteers seem to have had enough. I slept on duty, then breakfast of bacon, egg, toast, marmalade and tea.

16 January

Off 09:00 back on 23:00. Mrs Grellier and Mrs Dent, both full-time Civil Defence staff, went to bed again without permission. Played chess with Langton until 04:00.

17 January

Off 09:00 back on duty 23:00. I am reading *The Pickwick Papers*.

19 January

Went to Deptford Central Library. They have a very nice new girl there, good looking. She tells me she went to Addey and Stanhope School [*New Cross*]. On 17:00–23:00.

20 January

I was on 17:00–23:00 again. Langton told off Mrs Grellier and Mrs Dent for going out without permission. Paymaster-Commander Lee, deputy A.R.P. controller of Camberwell came in very, very drunk and incapable dressed in polo kit. He telephoned the one-armed Manning, the controller. I stood by to cut him off if there should be an alert. He appeared to think he was in command of a Navy ship. It snowed.

Sunday, 21 January

More snow. Pipes froze in lavatory at home. On 17:00–23:00.

22 January

More snow. I played chess with Langton, who bought me a cup of hot soup from the canteen, which he has done before. He is quite highly paid, an accountant for the borough. Snow is still on the ground.

24 January

On 17:00–23:00. I have finished reading *Pickwick* and started on *The Case of the Leaning Man*, by Christopher Bush.

I heard that Doug has begun work at Camberwell five days a week, 08:00–18:00, with an hour for lunch at 30/- a week.

25 January

Had a day off. Went to Auntie's early for the day. She gave me the cost of the correspondence course to return to my post office account. I repaid Dad the 9/3d I owed him. Uncle John called in at Norbury whilst I was there, which was nice. Snow.

26 January

09:00–17:00. Went to see Doug in evening. He works at Edwards High Vacuum Pump Works in Vaughan Road SE 5 now. Snow again.

27 Saturday

09:00–17:00. Very boring. I read the whole of John Langdon Davies' *Air Raid*. More snow.

28 Sunday

09:00–17:00. There is to be an arrangement whereby the lucky blighters still working in the libraries will do an occasional shift for us exploited library folk in the control centre. In evening, at home we all sat reading.

29 January

09:00–17:00. Snow worse than ever, a tram froze to the points at Rye Lane, I walked from there and got to work by 09:35. I asked for some work to do as am so bored waiting. I wrote final rate demands by hand. Five new women came to work at the centre, all on my shift, sadly only two are girls.

30 January

09:00–17:00. Read Harry Edmonds *The Death Ship*. Canteen cook now makes nice cakes. Started reading *Death of the Heart* by Elizabeth Bowen. Then *The Sacred Flame* by Somerset Maugham. Snow again.

31 January

09:00–17:00. I did more final rate demands and checked and cast lists of receipts correctly. Langton was very pleased. Snow. Transport still in a very poor state. Thaw later in the day.

1 February

23:00–09:00. I bought Mother a birthday card and took her to Lewisham Gaumont as a birthday outing and saw *The Man in the Iron Mask*, excellent. Then work by 23:00.

2 February

Mum's 47th birthday, I will buy her a frock next payday. Breakfast at Town hall, 08:00. Two rashers of bacon, fried egg, fried bread, toast and marmalade, had three hours sleep last night. At home slept from 11:00–16:00. Back on duty at 23:00.

3 February

Received from Mr Corbett correspondence course lessons one and two. I played chess all night with Langton. Seven full games. The temporary girl working at the centre gets £2/9 per week.

5 February

Read Eugene O'Neill, *Ah Wilderness*.

6 February

Off at 09:00. Returned books to Deptford Central Library, fines 5d. Pretty girl would not let me off paying. Quite right. I slept a very short part of day. On again at 23:00.

7 February

Off 09:00, on 23:00. Slept three hours of day, then some librarianship study. On duty I was preparing a list for the mayor to present A.R.P. silver badges and against my name I wrote 'badge issued' and pocketed the thing. I now feel guilty about it, but I do not want to give up any more time, especially for a silly ceremony. Up and alert all night as Carter Street Police Station sent us a warning that the IRA were likely to bomb A.R.P. posts and centres, stupid Irish buggers.

8 February

Studied in morning and wrote to Auntie Emm. Dozed in afternoon. Went to see Doug in evening. I was in bed at home all night.

9 February

Studied in the morning. To work 17:00–23:00, wearing A.R.P. badge. I am reading *Sense and Sensibility*.

10 February

On 17:00–23:00. I set up exercises for volunteers and checked the results with them. Just before 23:00, Commander Lee came in very, very drunk, dressed in puttees, riding breeches, wearing a cape, a new beard and a monocle. I did not conceal my disgust.

11 February

On 17:00–23:00. I played chess with Langton. I put through practice messages as some of the volunteers are getting bored already.

12 February

17:00–23:00. In morning I borrowed John Buchan's *History of English Literature* from Deptford Library. Not one of the recommended books. We are now training sanitary inspectors (who are very short of their own work at present). They are to take over from the Finance Office staff (hopefully from me too, though this has not been mentioned).

13 February

It is the anniversary of my starting at Dulwich Library.

14 February

I have read *The Nut Brown Maid*, by Philip Lindsay, not bad and *Goodbye Mr. Chips* by James Hilton which was excellent.

15 February

I telephoned Mr Hahn chief borough librarian, complaining about my conditions of work in the control centre and the length of time that I had suffered these long hours underground, in artificial light and very bad air. I suggested that other library staff might take a turn. He implied that he thought that I didn't know there was a war on, but he would consider the problem.

Hahn is a dapper little man always immaculately dressed in a black suit with waistcoat and pin-stripe trousers, wing collar and bow tie, fawn-coloured spats and black patent leather shoes, black homburg hat and rolled umbrella. Summer and winter it is the same with the addition of an overcoat in winter.

He visits all his libraries weekly on foot or by bus although the borough boundaries stretch from Crystal Palace to Southwark and from Croydon to Deptford. He is reserved with junior staff but sometimes a wry smile escapes from beneath his moustache. He is of German descent but served in the British Army in the First War with distinction.

16 February

I studied for three hours. Gilman telephoned from Dulwich Library to say that Hahn had taken on three temporary girls to work there so it did not look as though I would escape from A.R.P. Damn!

17 February

Did casting of rates and indexed a rates book.

Sunday, 18 February

Wonder of wonders! Sherwood is doing my duty today. Off to Auntie's in the morning, had a lovely day and borrowed some of her books for my literature studies. She says that she will leave her books and bookcase to me, which makes me sad. She advised me not to make any more fuss with Hahn, but to use my time in study. Snow then rain.

19 February

On 09:00–17:00. I told the borough treasurer of my desire to return to library work and of my letter to Hahn. He was most surprised and assured me that I was indispensable in the control centre, but perhaps my hours were excessive. He would look into it and appreciated the work Langton had told him I did for his department so accurately. Later I had very sore throat and in evening I gargled with potash.

20 February

09:00–17:00. Gargled potash, felt dreadful and said I must have a couple of hours off. Went to see Hahn in my dying state. He was not hopeful as my work 'was in the national interest'. I saw Ferdie (Miss Bulpitt, one of my library seniors = Ferdinand the Bull), I moaned and she said that she could not imagine the library staff doing any of my duties in the control centre. I told her that Sherwood had done one duty on a Sunday and she said 'Of course he's a dear, in spite of being a bit of an old woman'…and she is really a very nice person…so that seemed to be that. Then I went back to the Town Hall and sought out the borough treasurer who said that there was a meeting of heads of Emergency Services and as I appeared to have had a very rough deal as to hours for such a long time, and was clearly suffering in health, he would put my case for return to the service.

By 16:00 he told me it was agreed for Monday, but I must work up to and including Sunday in the centre.

I telephoned Hahn, who was cross that I told him, (he did not know). The so-and-so said it must be Wells Way Library not Dulwich, as the girls should be in the libraries in areas less likely to be bombed. That was my nice Dulwich Library job down the drain. Damned old fool! He also said report at 09:00 on Monday at Wells Way, even though clearly my voice had nearly gone.

Sunday, 25 February

I pinned a cartoon up in the control centre, aptly by Lee, about bearded naval officers. Played lots of chess with Langton, we will miss each other's company. I suppose he is thirty-something years old.

A Librarian Again

26 February

A librarian again, albeit at Wells Way, North Camberwell, 09:00–18:30 with an hour and a half for lunch and an hour for tea, not bad after my slave labour! In spite of what Hahn said there is still one girl there — Daisy Springall, rough of speech, loud-voiced and patronising to the poor old dears, her neighbours, who use that branch library. The branch librarian, old Mr Courtney, is cheekily called Norman by

Daisy, at least when talking to me. He is a First World War veteran with a bad foot wound.

Wells Way Library (courtesy of Southwark Archives).

Mr Courtney limps to the bus and back but otherwise stays seated all the time reading in the downstairs room that serves as his office and our staff room. He is terribly well-spoken, a bachelor in his late 50's who lives with his mother and, (says Daisy), his mistress 'Auntie'. Probably not his mistress, I think. He speaks in an uninhibited vulgar way about Hahn and Wootton, etc. and he joked with me that the Hun shot him in the foot as he was running away, so he said, when your turn comes to fight, don't run away; strange jokey philosophy!

27 February

Worked 09:00–18:30. Home on tram to lunch. In the evening, I walked along the Old Kent Road to New Cross Gate in pouring wet, getting a tram there, as am hard up. Stupid of me, got soaked through.

28 February

09:00–13:00, half-day. Courtney loaned me one of his own books on English literature, which he had brought from home especially. Endured some ribbing from Daisy about studying, as I was in the Royal Air Force Volunteer Reserve, 'so it was a waste of time, wasn't it?' I am sure that she would like to be asked to go out with me as there does not seem to be any other male in her sights at present. Telephoned Hahn to say that I wished to work at Dulwich as I needed a reference library for my studies and my appointment had been to Dulwich. He sounded cross. Brenda is still there.

29 February

09:00–17:00. I have started eating at a 'men's dining room' on Canal Bank. The food is excellent, cooked and served by the man and wife who rent the place. It's very cheap, with large helpings. Hahn came in to say he was moving Elsie Taylor to Dulwich and Daisy Springall to Central, so I must stay at Wells Way. I said that I could not believe that any part of the borough of Camberwell was safer from bombing than any other and he said, 'You do not know about these things' and walked off. Letter from Auntie Emm. Borrowed several love stories for Mother.

1 March

09:30–18:30, Wells Way. Studied in evening and wrote correspondence course answers until 02:00. At least I learned at the control centre not to distinguish night and day but just to get on with work.

2 March

I posted correspondence course. One penny postage at printed paper rate unsealed. Hahn came in wearing his usual creamy-buff spats, black pin-stripe trousers, black jacket and waistcoat with gold fob-watch, black overcoat with small velvet collar, rolled umbrella. His little black moustache curled up in a smile as he said how pleased he was with my work; he relied on his young men to man vital services such as Wells Way Library, among the factories of north Camberwell. Silly old bugger.

Sunday, 3 March

My first Sunday totally off-duty in six months. We went to church together, where I was welcomed rather as a reformed backslider than as a chap who had not been able to attend because of Civil Defence shift work. Started reading J.B. Priestley *Four in Hand*.

4 March

Longer opening hours. This is what I'm really at Wells Way for, 13:00–20:30. Only three people came in after 18:30, so I labelled new books, dipping into some of them. This is better than the control centre, even though Hahn does not know it.

5 March

Wrote to Auntie Emm when I got home. I am reading Dorothy Sayers *Devil to Pay*.

6 March

09:00–12:00. Went to see Doug and played chess and had tea and biscuits. In evening I went to Dulwich Library to play table tennis against the air raid wardens there, as part of the library team with Brenda Halls (Bunny).

7 March

Wells Way. 09:00–17:00. Mother treated me to a circle seat at Lewisham Gaumont 2/- and ice-cream. *Babes in Arms*, it was very good.

8 March

Hours again extended, 13:30–21:00. Had to lock up as no porter. Damn and blast! There is a pair of enormous oak gates at the bottom of the steep steps, at road level. These have a chain and padlock.

9–12 March

The porter, Worth, is still off sick; he is to be summonsed for non-payment of rates. I expect he will be sacked. I locked up each night and on the 12th, a very dark night, my torch failed, making it damned difficult.

13 March

Drake is replacing Worth. Stocktaking.

14 March

09:00–17:00. Snow and sleet again. Doug over in the evening planning Easter ramble. Chess. Wrote to Auntie, bought via Glaishers:- W.C. Berwick Sayers *Introduction to Library Classification* 10/6d. less 1/- discount.

17 March

After lunch to Doug's. We played chess. Very nice tea, played whist and invasion, no church this week!

19 March

13:00–21:00. Hahn came in and questioned me about the way Wells Way Library was run. I was able to say that we kept a periodicals register, (did not say that I had just started it). He asked about stocktaking and was not very satisfied by my evasive answers. He criticised the dusty shelves.

20 March

I washed some shelves in soap and hot water whilst Courtney went out to buy a ledger book to serve as a withdrawals register, at my suggestion. He then entered some of the withdrawn titles. A start anyway! I agreed with his suggestion that Hahn need not know that one had not been kept in the past.

Hahn then came in and criticised dusty shelves and asked Courtney if he kept a withdrawals register and Courtney smiled his disarming smile and said, 'Good Lord, yes, indeed.' Courtney paid for my lunch the next day.

22 March

It was Good Friday. I went on a ramble with Doug. 09:20 train, Brockley to Merstham, 2/4d returned from Leatherhead, 3d excess fare. Excellent ramble, weather fair and dull.

23 March

Haircut 5d. Buns for tomorrow 6d. Fine day.

Easter Day, 24 March

Dodged church. Ramble with Doug. Nunhead to Sevenoaks, 2/8d return. Wet underfoot. Spent 3/10d.

25 March

Easter bank holiday Monday. I get them off now! Went to Auntie's and had a good time. We played cards.

26 March

13:00–21:00. Am restricting expenditure this week to 4/- to pay for rambles.

27 March

Now on 10:00–13:00. Hahn came in as the padlock on external gates was stolen during the night. HE ASKED WHY IT WAS NOT TAKEN IN AT NIGHT, I heard him! Courtney said, 'Well sir, actually it was securing the gates' and then he burst out laughing, for which he thought it diplomatic to apologise.

30 March

09:00–17:00. At lunchtime paid £1 into Post Office Savings bank account, balance is now £3. Studied in the evening.

Sunday, 31 March

Went to church in the evening only. Did some study. I am reading C.S. Forrester, *Flying Colours* so I should prefer to be a sailor now! Repaired wireless, needs one new accumulator soon.

4 April

Worked evening. Went with Mum and Dad to visit Uncle Jack [*Homewood*] and Auntie Vi at Mottingham.

Sunday, 7 April

I spent the day, 09:00–17:00, on duty in the control centre as volunteer standing in for Ferdie (Bulpitt). Left her a note asking her to see that my name did not get on to the rota for regular relief as I had done so much more than my fair share, full-time. A pleasant surprise because Brenda was on with me standing in for someone else so the time passed very quickly. I was at the controller's phone. It did not ring. Went to see Doug in evening.

19 April

Ida's birthday. I gave her 5/-. I am reading Dodie Smith *Three Plays: Autumn Crocus, Service and Touch Wood.*

20 April

Lunchtime went to Rye Lane and bought two shirts, two pairs of socks and one pair of braces for exactly £1.

29 April

My salary is now £105 p.a. [*per annum*] and I shall raise Mum's £1 per week to 24/-. Paid £1/1 into P.O. account, balance now £3/6. Played chess with Doug several evenings lately.

5 May

Sunday revision school at Chaucer House, 12:30–19:30.

10 May

Invasion of Belgium, Holland and Luxembourg. Incendiary bombs fell near Canterbury.

12 May

Whit Sunday, I dodged church. Went on ramble with Doug. Nunhead to Sevenoaks, 2/11d Lovely day, total cost 4/4d.

13 May

Bank holiday cancelled. Work as usual.

15 May

Worked 09:00–12:00, then on to Norbury to see Auntie. We went to Williamson's for lunch and walked to the Rookery, Streatham Common, which was very pretty. Tea at the Rookery and returned to Norbury for wireless news bulletin and supper. Auntie gave me a bottle of blood tonic for my spots and £1 towards the cost of any books for study, as a birthday present. She is generous.

16 May

I worked 09:00–17:00, then went to Dulwich after work to see Brenda and return some books. I had a long talk with her, whilst she worked on the issue desk, mostly about politics and theatre. She wants to go into theatre like others in her family.

22 May

Dad is calling me at 06:15 each weekday to study. I bought a new bottle of blood tonic. Hours 09:00–18:00.

23 May

Oswald Moseley and his fascist gang have been arrested. He should be shot, but we have become too soft. Auntie sent me an extra 10/- birthday money to spend on myself not on study books.

Sunday, 26 May

I did volunteer control centre duty for Biggs who badly wanted to visit a school friend now in the Army. I took correspondence course work with me.

27 May

Am working same hours. Dad is now calling me at 06:00 for study. Mum gave me £1 birthday present, towards a raincoat. Drake's cigarette caused a small fire in the staff area, two good cushions burnt. He put it out himself and is much chastened. I had an extra section fitted to my gas mask for additional protection. I took it to Post 21 in Camberwell, where the man in charge was very friendly when I told him that I worked in the control centre. He showed me how to fit and work a gas helmet for babies, which might prove useful.

31 May

On at 13:00, so went to Lewisham in the morning and bought a raincoat for 25/-.

Sunday, 2 June

Had ramble with Doug. Train Brockley to Boxhill 2/11d return, cheap day. Lovely day, excellent walk, total cost 4/11d Trains all delayed for military purposes. Got home just before midnight.

TODAY 26,256 MEN WERE LIFTED FROM THE BEACHES OF DUNKIRK. IT IS THE SEVENTH DAY OF THE EVACUATION OF OUR FORCES AND THERE ARE ONLY TWO MORE DAYS OPEN TO US.

6 June

Took out a £50 War Loan Assurance with the Prudential at 5/6d a week for 15 years. It will cost £55/5.

Sunday, 9 June

Doug came down for cards and chess.

10 June

Italy came into the war against us. Not very important we think.

17 June

France surrendered.

23 June

My hours the same. Doug came to tea and we took photographs and developed them in my bedroom.

25 June

Air raid warning from 13:00–16:00. We got up and sat in the kitchen away from the window. We do not have a shelter.

26 June

I began repainting the scullery after work.

27 June

Doug came 19:30, and we printed out the film that we had developed.

8 July.

To Auntie's to stay, as a holiday for the next two weeks. Did some correspondence course work. With Auntie to the Couratins at 49 Playfield Crescent, Dulwich, to tea. They also had other visitors, also friends of Auntie's, we had an excellent time.

Sunday, 14 July

Met Doug from Auntie's at East Croydon Station for a good ramble Merstham—Leatherhead. Barricades everywhere out of town, such as aeroplane obstacles in flat fields.

15 July

Auntie and I had intended to go to Hampton Court, but it poured, so we went to Richmond on the bus and had a lovely lunch for 1/9d each in the Cadena Restaurant and then we went to the flicks.

16 July

I painted the inside of Auntie's bedroom windows with anti-shatter paint (a rubber and varnish solution). She has now at last agreed to accept the Wigleys' next-door offer to go down their garden (Anderson) shelter, when warnings are given. They told me that they were very worried about her otherwise, because of her age (75).

18 July

To the Rex at Norbury, with Auntie to see *The Dark Command* about the American Civil War.

19 July

The Couratins came to tea. Very good, I helped get it ready. Auntie gave me a quarter of a pound of tea towards our library tea club.

Sunday, 21 July

End of a very nice holiday at Norbury with Auntie, in spite of a lot of rain. Home by 21:00. Heard that Ida is engaged to Alvin, a Canadian soldier, the twerp, and is to be married in the autumn. A selfish dream decision that will worry Mum and Dad. I told her that I would not get serious with a girl until after the war, in case I got killed, and Alvin might get killed and that I thought that the £1 a week that she paid Mother was not enough as I gave her 24/- a week.

24 July

I bought Dad an ounce of tobacco as Ida has depressed him immensely. Hours of work remain the same Kilbey and Biggs both accepted as air crew, perhaps I can manage to get in as ground crew, and my eyesight is not all that short.

Syd at this time.

25 July

Doug came in the evening. We printed some more snaps.

26 July

I was on at one. In the morning I went to New Cross to be measured for my first made-to-measure suit, it will be five guineas, blue pin-stripe, to be paid for by instalments. New shoes 19/11d.

30 July

I now get a cost of living wage bonus. We heard a low-flying plane at 22:00. Searchlights and machine-gun fire down the searchlight beam, which went out.

1 August

Eggs are very scarce now and Mr De Laiche gets two dozen every now and again for Courtney, who so far has sold me three separate half-dozens for Mum at 1/4d a time. I bought 100 walnuts for Mum for pickling from a greengrocer in Wells Way. She began pickling them that evening, pricking them and sprinkling them with salt laid out on a tray. I went up to Doug's later for chess.

Sunday, 4 August

I had a ramble with Doug. Military police would not let us leave the train at Swanley as our purpose was only walking. We went on to Otford and paid 1/3d excess on our 2/- fare. Lovely day, Chelsfield, Knockholt, Chevening, Otford and Shoreham.

5 August

Bank holiday cancelled.

6 August

Half a dozen eggs from De Laiche. Doug came in evening and we developed our ramble film.

9 August

Sollis, the grocer next door to the library, sold me one egg for 3d.

10 August

13:30–21:00. Another egg from Sollis. In the morning, I tried on my new suit at New Cross; a perfect fit.

12 August

Sollis sold me half a dozen eggs.

15 August

On 09:00–17:00. Bought six eggs from Courtney, 1/4d. To Doug's in evening. We messed about with their typewriter. Air raid warning: 19:20–19:35, we took no notice as no sound of planes or guns. One hundred and forty-four enemy planes down today. Croydon bombed with the warning coming 10 minutes after the first bombs. Houses reported damaged there, I do hope that Auntie is safe.

16 August

On 13:30–21:00. Received *Cataloguing Rules: Author and Title Entry*, by first parcel post. Warning alarm 12:20–13:10. I was 10 minutes late for work. Another warning 17:50–18:15 so we closed the library for that time.

17 August

Saturday, on 13:30–21:00.

Sunday, 18 August

At home. We heard hundreds of planes flying high overhead between 13:10 and 13:15 and the wireless went dead and then the sirens sounded. We heard planes diving and gunfire. All clear at 14:00. Fire engines later as the coal wharf on fire. Another warning 17:50–18:10.

22 August

On until 17:00. Doug came to tea and I gave him *Oxford Book of English Prose* for his birthday. I got half a dozen eggs for Mother. In the night Ida awakened me, saying that she had lain awake from about 02:30 (it was then 03:30), listening to planes and gunfire and seeing flares and searchlights. We all then got up as firing got heavy from the railway at the back and planes were overhead. Warning followed at 03:40 until 04:00.

23 August

On 13:30–21:00.

24 August

Working from 09:00–17:00. Air raid warning, 20:15–21:15. Got to work by 09:40 by walking most of the way. Air raid 15:45–16:47, heavy explosions, Large number of planes and heavy gunfire in distance. Night warning, and there was heavy bombing of the city from 23:30–01:30.

25 August

I went to see Auntie Emm and stayed with her until 21:00. Air raid warnings, 22:40–23:30 and 00:40–01:00. I stayed in bed but later got up and went downstairs, with heavy barrage overhead. I had a look, made tea, then went back to bed as we have no protection anyway.

26 August

On 13:00–21:00. Air raid warning 15:20–16:00. At night, 21:30–03:40. With guns, planes searchlights and bombs.

27 August

On 13:00–21:00. Night warnings, 21:28–23:50 and 00:30–01:50. Distant planes, bombs and guns.

28 August

On from 09:00–12:00, whilst bombs were dropping around me in Camberwell and at Dulwich and Bermondsey. Night warning from 20:58–04:50 guns, bombs, flares. Woolworths in the Old Kent Road hit opposite Albany Road, incendiary bombs on adjoining shops. Also, the cold storage plant in Albany Road, Spa Road, Bermondsey, Dog Kennel Hill,

Warner Road and Loughborough Road, all hit with high explosive bombs. There is heavy damage and casualties.

*Bomb damage at Arica Road Brockley
(courtesy Lewisham Heritage Centre, Lewisham Council).*

29 August

09:00–17:00. Doug's birthday. First full night's sleep for a long time.

30 August

On 13:00–21:00. Air raid 11:45–12:35, 15:25–15:35 and 16:40–17:50. Night raid 21:10–03:50.

31 August

Air raid warnings 08:30–09:00, 10:45–11:20, 13:00–14:00, 17:50–19:20 (saw a dogfight over the docks), 21:45–22:25, 23:30–00:50 and 01:00–03:55. Work 13:30–21:00.

Sunday, 1 September

To Doug's for tea and chess. Day air raid warnings, 11:00–11:35, 13:45–14:47. A night's sleep.

2 September

On 13:00–21:00. Air raid warnings, 08:10–08:50, 16:27–17:50 and 22:45–02:55. I have a nasty head cold.

3 September

The war has been on one year now. I was on at Wells Way, 13:00–21:00. Air raids, 10:25–11:30, 14:50–16:00 and 1:40–23:50.

4 September

On 09:00–13:00. Air raid warnings 09:15–09:50, 13:20–13:50 and 21:50–22:50.

5 September

Working from 09:00–17:00. Air raid warnings were on and off all day and all night.

6 September

On 13:00–21:00. Air raid warnings on and off most of day and night. A very bad night at Brockley, by which time I advised that we should go and find a shelter and it was too late to try. We crouched flat on the kitchen floor. Whistle of very close bombs, shatteringly loud explosions as Brockley Road received a stick of bombs. Heavy damage from Brockley up to the Elephant and Castle. Camberwell's Peckham Park Road Depot was hit, but the Old Kent Road Gas Works was a near miss.

Many years later, on visiting Lewisham Local Studies to check war damage records, John noted: "6 September: the first three bombs in the borough at 102 Tyrwhitt Rd, Breakspears Road *and Brockley Road. On the 7th 136 incidents in Deptford, including the first unexploded bomb."*

Air raid damage to the back of 67 Breakspears Rd (courtesy Lewisham Heritage, Lewisham Council).

7 September

On duty at Wells Way Library, 13:00–21:00. Air raids 17:00–17:40. Mass air attack on the Surrey Docks, Old Kent Road Gas Works and all down south of the river the docks on fire with blazes close to the library. Heavy explosions continually, close by, so I went to bring Mr Sollis and his young family from his shop to shelter in the library basement until I shut early at 20:31 just after the all-clear. The sirens went off again 10 minutes later. Screaming bombs were dropping around Havil Street just after I passed down it, walking home.

The fire illuminated all London, with the bloody Hun stoking it from continuous waves of bombers. This raid continued until 05:00.

I reached home at 02:15 after many dives into doorways and lying down in the roadway once or twice. I had to divert around the larger incidents and areas with unexploded bombs, as the police would not let me through.

Yesterday 400 were killed in South London and there were 1,300 serious injuries.

Sunday, 8 September

Air raid 12:30–13:20. The people in the crowded shelters last night apparently behaved very well. Firemen went into the docks area and died in numbers, fires are still blazing there. Old Kent Road Gasworks fire was put out today. We all went to shelter under the railway arch at Brockley

Cross. Dad rather reluctant, stiff upper lip? We found 'regulars' there, who had the best places. I don't think we will come again.

9 September

On duty 13:00–21:00. Trams from Brockley to the Marquis of Granby only. An unexploded delayed-action bomb at New Cross. I had to get off at Vesta Road and walk over the hill to New Cross Fire Station, where I got a tram to Havil Street and then walked. Houses along my whole route are severely damaged. Gimber's Tub Works, Peckham Steam Laundry and Anderson's empty building are completely gutted. Gas and telephone out of action at Wells Way Library. Courtney says that the bombs near him in Dulwich last night were filled with tar and creosote and all caused fires. Warnings from 17:00–18:30 and 20:45–05:45.

St Catherine's parish church at Hatcham was hit by fire bomb. Father is a friend of the vicar and did what he could to help him.

10 September

On the way to work, delayed-action bombs were still going off in Brockley, and in Peckham Road a whole row of shops near Sam's Furniture shop were completely flat, with rescue squads still busy trying to get out people trapped beneath. My hours are now 13:00–19:30 to assist staff in getting home.

Coming home there was machine-gunning overhead as I got to Havil Street. People started running, but there was nowhere to run to. I walked a poor old lady to a shelter in Brunswick Square, talking to her about walking in Kent; she said 'God Bless' as I left her there. Raid warning 12:50–13:15. Raids also from 16:50–17:15, 17:20–17:45, 18:00–18:25 and 20:15–04:55.

12 September

On from 09:00–17:00. Taking glass splinters out of the spines of books. Worth, who has been missing, has resigned. Courtney says it's a case of the shits, by which he means he has the wind-up or neurasthenia as the council's doctor's letter states. It's peculiar as he was in the Navy during the last war. Warnings sounded 16:45–17:40 and 21:00 until 05:50. We lay awake in our beds however.

13 September

I must keep my fingers crossed today! Wells Way, 09:00–19:00. No porter so I must lock up. Air raid warnings 19:40–08:35, 09:45–14:00, 15:55–16:10, and 21:00–05:45. We lay mostly awake in our beds.

14 September

Dulwich Library re-opened after war damage. Livesey Library blown up by high explosive bomb, with façade still standing. Inside are two firebombs that finished it off. Harry Davis went back to work there the morning after, salvaging books and began to modify his pacifist views. Raids 9:25–9:50, 15:50–17:15, 18:00–18:40, 19:50–21:00 and 21:40–03:45

I slept heavily between waking periods.

Sunday, 15 September

Air raids 12:00 noon to 12:55 and 14:15–15:20.

16 September

Wells Way Library, 09:00–19:00 Galvin our new porter (from the Livesey). There were raids all day with short intervals. Raid all night without a break. Oh Lord, how long?

17 September

Worked same hours. Raids all day with intervals, all night without cease. Parachute mines in Lewisham.

18 September

Raids all day with intervals, all night without cease until dawn. Some unexploded bombs are said to bear British markings and the official explanation is that they were left behind at Dunkirk.

19 September

Raids all day with intervals and all night continuously till dawn. Unholy bang as we dozed under the kitchen table, we were thrown into one heap. Mantle Road School, opposite was hit by high explosive bomb, all our front windows and the glass in the front door blown in. Glass splinters everywhere, soot and mortar came down chimney onto our blankets. The air was choking. The cats not too bothered. We are unhurt, thank God.

[*The* London County Council Bomb Damage Maps of London 1939–1945 *show St Norbert Road as a mixture of 'seriously damaged—repairable at a cost' and 'general blast damage—not structural'.*]

20 September

On from 09:00–19:00. Siren sounded about 09:00 in the morning, but I continued on in the tram, got out at Camberwell Town Hall and there was a terrific barrage going up and hundreds of planes going over. Shrapnel from the nearest guns was whistling down, so I stood behind the baffle wall of the Town Hall entrance with several other folk until the gunfire eased off a bit, then I walked on to Wells Way Library.

We had an all-clear later, though a plane was fired at and jettisoned a bomb. They also dropped a parachute mine measuring nine feet six inches long and two feet six inches in circumference on Dundalk Road Brockley, near our house. It did not go off, and wearing my Civil Defence armband and badge, I was allowed to go and see it, early next morning. Some of the landmines work on the magnetic principal and can be set off by a vehicle passing of or by the spades of the rescue squads. Raid all night until dawn.

21 September.

My hours were 09:00–19:00. Raids with intervals all day and all night till dawn.

[*Three landmines fell of which only one exploded. Two-thousand people were made temporarily homeless.*]

Sunday, 22 September

Soon after 05:00, I was in bed upstairs and dozing uneasily when a delayed-action bomb went off at the back of the house, our back windows were blown in and a chimney collapsed, several neighbours' houses became unsafe, and needed propping up.

Just before 13:00 we were turned out of the house and told we could not return for several hours. We took our roast dinner out of the oven and walked with it, and the cats and our best clothes to Mrs Green's at 91, Endwell Road, where Grandad has rooms.

Five naval men eventually removed the detonator of the Dundalk Road mine and we were able to reheat the dinner for 16:00 back home, at our own risk, as there was a raid on and gunfire, they said could set off the enormous amount of unstable high explosive in the mine. It was emptied and removed by 20:00.

23–28 September

Hours at Wells Way now 09:00–18:00. Raids with intervals every day and most of every night. I bought Dad an ounce of Shag 1/6d. Bought Doug as birthday present *The Oxford Book of English Verse*.

29 September–11 October

Hours 09:00–18:00, Mondays to Saturdays, with Wednesday closing at 12:00.

11–16 October

Night raids ending around 02:00. Sleeping rest of night.

17 October

Violent all-night raid, 19:00–07:00. New Cross Gate Station Bridge hit.

18 October

Walked over the hill to New Cross Gate to get tram and ditto in reverse to come home for several days.

22 October

Johnny Hahn came in at lunchtime to tell us to close the library at 18:00 until further notice and that thenceforth we would be employed on billeting the homeless, as the rest centres (in school and church halls) were all full up. Just in time Mr Hards came in and sold me a bottle of port for 1/11d.

Housing the Homeless

Next, I worked in Camberwell Billeting Office, re-housing bombed-out homeless people, it required tact as some had suffered bereavement, some were recovering from injuries and were in shock. Most had to make do with rooms in large houses in Dulwich, which were mansions that the very wealthy had left empty on fleeing London for safer places. Many of these people came from the communities of close-knit families of North Peckham, Camberwell, the Old Kent Road, etc. Some had always been very poor and they were horrified at being out in an enormous cold room (one room per family sharing kitchen and bathroom) in what to them were remote, out of the way, parts of their borough. One of my duties was to travel round the borough in cars that doubled as rescue vehicles, having a stretcher affixed to the roof, seeking out empty properties that a sanitary inspector or a rate collector had already identified as of possible use to us and affixing to the front door a requisition notice. A tough bloke was sent with me to break open front or back door as required.

23 October

To the Town Hall for instruction in billeting work, but back to Canal Bank 'dining rooms' for lunch. They were pleased to see me and gave me even larger portions, whilst a raid was in progress and some people left hurriedly.

24 October

Control Centre friends said that bombs were falling in Canal Bank area so I decided not to go to lunch but fasted.

25 October

Am billeting the homeless now 09:00–17:00 each day with Sundays off. We sleep under the kitchen table every night now, illogically feeling exposed in the windowless bedrooms. We have boarded up the kitchen window with wood that used to hold back the coal in the coal cellar.

[On 27 October Ida married Alvin McLaughlin, a Canadian soldier and they lived at Redhill.]

28 October

Letter from Auntie Emm informing us that Uncle John and Aunt Kate had been bombed out of Whitford Gardens, Mitcham, and that they had taken themselves off to 36, Station Road, Marlow, Bucks. I advised Auntie Emm, by return to let them know that they could claim 5/- each a week billeting allowance to help pay for their Marlow lodgings as they could both be termed aged, but that they would need to get Mitcham Town Hall people to certify that they had been bombed out of their home address.

29 October

Auntie Emm was bombed out at 01:00. She was in the dining room under the table and although the French windows were blown in, frame and all, across her body, she came out safely, thank God.

Bomb damage to numbers 67 and 69 Breakspears Road (courtesy Lewisham Heritage, Lewisham Council).

30 October

I have persuaded the billeting officer that I must have a half-day off tomorrow to help Auntie, as the brother who would help had also been bombed out and had gone away.

1 November

Work 09:00–13:00. Then I went on to Norbury by trams. The bomb was in Southbrook Road. There is very bad damage to Auntie's house. She would insist on working with me at clearing up and storing things stacked against inside walls in the front rooms, up and down. We were then able to lock those rooms. All of the back windows and doors were blown out, including the whole frame of the French windows. All backroom ceilings down, mess as I expected, soot and plaster over all.

I took her up to town via several trams and put her on the 17:30 train from Euston to Carlisle, she should be there by early Saturday morning. She is truly a brave old English lady, all on her own in her distress. Dad was on duty so he couldn't come. She had pitifully few belongings with her. I know we both thought that we would not see each other again.

When I left Auntie as her train drew out, I got a Tube train to the Oval and then two trams home. Auntie put in my care a bed-warmer and a parcel of jellies, biscuits, sugar and tea from her bombed larder, and asked me to deliver it to her friend, Mrs Agnes Samuels, 309, Baring Road Lee, whenever I could. I had been to Baring Road once or twice with Auntie. Agnes Samuels had been a supply teacher, as she had married and had children. Her husband was a retired Cunard Liner captain and she had had lots of trips with him.

Sunday, 3 November

The first night for 56 nights without a raid. Delivered the bed-warmer and the food parcel to the Samuels' for Auntie.

4 November

Raids again. Read Priestley's *Let the People Sing*.

5 November

Dad and I went to Norbury and moved some of the stuff out of the kitchenette, which was otherwise totally unprotected. We locked it into the drawing room. Also moved all her books out of the bookcase into the drawing room, lots of them still have glass splinters sticking out of their spines, no time to attend to them. The house will now be boarded up.

We then went into May and Philpot, 1536, London Road, Norbury and arranged for a surveyor to assess the war damage to Auntie's house. To come next Tuesday at 15:00. Fee in advance (I suppose in case we are killed).

We also managed to get the Patent Steam Carpet Beating Company at Thornton Heath to collect the large Indian carpet from the back bedroom for cleaning (soot and plaster) after Dad and I got the rest of the glass splinters out of it, estimated cost of cleaning 12/-.

7–27 November

Hours the same. Bed under the table.

11 November

Poppies sold as usual. Received a letter from Auntie with a £5/5cheque to meet my expenses, surveyor's fee, carpet cleaning, fares, etc.

12 November

I scrounged time off in afternoon to get to meet the surveyor at Norbury. Mrs Samuels had let me know that she needs the flex for the bed-warmer, so I found it in the debris at Colebrook Road. The woman must think that my life is a gentle picnic!

Bad night for bombs, back and front. Patched windows crashed in. Wind blowing straight through the house so not much sleep.

[Later in life, John checked the index of damaged housing held at Lewisham Central Library. There were five entries for 21 St Norbert Rd. The first was 12 November and read 'slight damage'.]

13 November

Wrote to Auntie.

16 November

To get to work now my regular route is tram from Brockley Cross to the Marquis of Granby, then I walk to New Cross Gate over the bombed New Cross Gate Bridge, wait half an hour for a bus which goes through the side streets of New Cross and Peckham to Harders Road and then a tram to Camberwell.

Sunday, 17 November

Ida and Mac (Alvin McLaughlin) came to visit us, from 16:15–17:30 (no longer in case a raid should start!).

18 November

Posted the flex to Mrs Samuels.

28 November

Hours now 09:00–16:15 allowing something for travel difficulties.

29 November

A heavy night raid.

30 November

Gave Dad 5/- for his birthday, nothing to buy in the shops.

2 December

Ida and Mac came to tea after I had worked 10:00–14:00. Received two letters from Auntie and one from the surveyor, who has assessed her damage much too low at £140, so I shall have to chase him up.

4 December

I bought a leather wallet after work at Gulliver's, Peckham, Dad's Christmas present to me, 4/11d.

7 December

No raid tonight.

Sunday, 8 December

Went to tea at Doug's with raid whilst we ate. Played chess. Still very heavy gunfire and bombs when I went down the road at 21:30.

9 December

No warnings. I sent off Auntie's War Damage Claim as amended after further discussion with the surveyor. Went to bed under the table every night.

Sunday, 15 December

Doug to tea.

18 December

Auntie Emm's birthday. Gave Alvin 25 cigs as Christmas present.

21 December

Dad and I patched up the downstairs front windows (again) and brought my desk downstairs from my bedroom. Sent Auntie *Memory Hold The Door*, from us all.

23 December

On from 09:00–16:15. Went to see Sollis in his boarded-up shop and he sold me six eggs for Christmas, 2/-. Night raid, they hit the Railway Tavern, New Cross.

25 December

Ida and Mac came.

27 December

Bad raid locally. In Breakspears Road a land mine exploded. New Cross Synagogue and tram depot Aspinall's paint works all went down. Incendiary on Deptford Town Hall.

29 December

Very bad raid on city of London all on fire.

1941

I began the year still billeting the bombed-out families, but now operating from Goldsmith's L.C.C. School, Southampton Way, Camberwell.

1 January

I settled 34 people in requisitioned premises during my 09:00–16:30 stint. The next day it was 40 people.

3 January

I settled 70 people.

5 January

Fifty people settled. We are sleeping regularly under the kitchen table, at least it is warm. I often have lunch with colleagues at Queen's Cafe, a two-course hot meal costing 1/10d. Library assistants gather from various war jobs to which they are allocated.

A tweedy Scotch woman with plain face, has been appointed supervisor of re-housing, from outside London, she will be appalled at how we have to exist! They have nearly completed bricking up the window hole under which I sit to work, perhaps I shall soon have less noise and dust.

9 January

Bomb removed from front of library opposite, buses and trams restarted.

10 January

Another delayed-action bomb found at the Central Library opposite. We were given the option to ignore it, which we did, although others in Ondine Road and Beauville Road went off, so we were lucky.

Camberwell Central Library was large and well-stocked with 35,000 books, as well as a music library and an excellent reference library (1920s Guide to the Borough of Camberwell).

11 January

Saturday night, Camberwell Central Library was burnt out, with great loss of books, many unique. I was working on Sunday, so I went across the road, as I thought on my way to lunch, to look at the wrecked building, but instead I was impelled to assist in retrieving a few dozen books, but piled hundreds of charred ones for removal. We have settled 1,111 people in requisitioned premises so far.

13 January

I went to Oliver Goldsmith's School, as usual. Although the bomb in front of the library has been defused, there are still bombs at the side and rear. I hope that they are not ticking away.

I ducked under the ropes when I had a brief lunch break and inspected the library. The newsroom roof has collapsed, the whole place is gutted. The reference library is badly damaged, so sad to lose all those valuable books, but better than losing people. The junior library is almost totally burned out and the whole building will probably have to be taken down.

I looked down the crater at the front, it was enormous and of great depth. In the afternoon I told Sherwood what I had been up to and he said he was surprised that I was such a daring bugger on the quiet. He told me that Hahn had said that there were no firewatchers in the building. They had fled to shelter elsewhere when the bombs began to whistle down, thus we lost the Central Library.

14 January

They are looking for somewhere else for us to work. The bricking up of the window places was not for our benefit, but to prepare the building as another rest centre for the bombed-out. I had lunch in the Town Hall basement canteen. We have been sitting near two delayed-action high explosive bombs at the library ruin opposite. They were dug out and steamed today.

15 January

I came home all the way by tram as they have made a temporary bridge over the railway at New Cross Gate Station. There are now small sandbags everywhere in Deptford propped against each lamppost for use in smothering incendiary bombs.

17 January

I was driven in a stretcher car to the Rolls Estate Office in the Old Kent Road to present personally to the manager an official requisition for some of their unoccupied little flats and houses in the side streets. So many people would rather stay in the area they know, however blasted. I was not well received.

23 and 24 January

Very busy. No raids.

25 January

My day off for the month. I went to Deptford Library. I am reading *Polycarp's Progress*, by Victor Canning. I am to start having Sundays off, working only Mondays to Saturdays.

1 February

I went out in the stretcher car visiting families re-housed in requisitioned premises to collect rents.

2 February

Mum's birthday, gave her 5/- and a card. Ida and Mac visited.

6 February

Haircut 9d. New toothbrush 7½d. Wrote to Ida and to Auntie.

10 February

Auntie sent me 15/-. I went out in the stretcher car to the North Camberwell area collecting rents. It was sad to see such heavy damage in the Wells Way Cottage Green area. I will have known many of the people as library users.

17 February

Heavy bombing again at night in the Evelina Road and Peckham Park Road area.

23 February

Bombs in Oglander Road, Arnott Road, Nutbrook Street, Denby Street, Bellenden Road, Peckham Rye, etc.

24 February

We dealt with the shocked homeless from last night. We have an incident list of course. I sent off for the Library Association entrance examination fee. My shoes were re-heeled for 2/-.

27 February

No raid tonight.

28 February

Thank God! Dad started as full-time PAID air raid warden, he, of all people should at least be paid for what he does. He has been a volunteer and has had lots of courses. He is appointed to Dundalk Road Post (two streets from home in Oldman the builder's yard). [*Post number 17 on junction of Dundalk and Avignon Roads*].

> Metropolitan Borough of Deptford
>
> ## Civil Defence
>
> ### This is to certify that
>
> Mr. S. Teague.
>
> was a member of the WARDENS Service in the
> (Whole-time)
> Civil Defence Organisation of the Borough of Deptford
> from   28.2.41.   to   1.7.45.
>
> *Ernest A. Fields*
>
> *Town Clerk and A.R.P. Controller.*
>
> Date   28th June, 1945.

7 March

Our housing office was moved to the Amalgamated Engineering Union Headquarters in Peckham Road. We have been told that we will not have access to their air raid shelter which is the only deep one that I know of, as we have only requisitioned part of the offices. Sherwood insisted that we start by polishing the desks, Oh God, how strange! With all the blast it will be dusty again in a few hours. He means well and pretends the war does not exist, being cheerful towards our poor homeless folk, but a veteran with one leg is excused his oddness.

He wears an aluminium leg fitted to his stump high up on the thigh. It was fitted with an articulated knee joint. He is often in considerable pain. One day in the staffroom we were alone together and I asked why the knee joint could not be adjusted to prevent the continual tearing of his trousers. I had chosen a bad day. He was in dreadful pain and cried out '*Oh Christ*'. He said it did not matter a damn about the trousers and the joint and there and then he took off the leg and showed me the ulcerated stump. I grew up by a few years instantly.

The next day he had to go to Roehampton for treatment. He rode an ancient bicycle the short distance from home to work going home for lunch. He smoked heavily to ease his pain (not at work of course), his face was heavily lined and he was prematurely grey. He is married with children and his name is Leslie.

8 March

A big blitz night. A.R.P. Centre and Women's Voluntary Service also moved into A.E.U. with us, from 25, Camberwell Grove.

Sunday, 9 March

Heavy blitz on Camberwell.

10 and 11 March

Housing Saturday's victim-survivors.

15 March

The Camberwell bombs are in Grove Park, Grove Lane, Bushey Hill Road, Lyndhurst Way and Kirkwood Road.

Sunday, 16 March

Day Off. I went on a ramble with Doug. Leatherhead Station, Bookham, Stoke D'Abernon etc. 3/- fare.

18 March

I explained my job to the newly-appointed chief billeting officer, Selkirk Chapman, who will be in a reserved occupation here when I join the R.A.F. for active service!

19 March

A night raid, which was a terrible experience as I was on fire duty all night on the roof of the A.E.U. building in Peckham, and I could see the explosions and fires in the direction of Brockley. Dad was involved in going to the aid of casualties in the bombing of flats at the top of our road, where many were killed. [*Syd knew some of the people whose bodies he pulled from the wreckage of their homes.*]

20 March

Dad very quiet before going off on duty. I paid 1/6d to the Red Cross.

'It is of the Lord's mercy that we are not consumed, because his compassion faileth not.' Reverend Bamford sent me this text, but what about the other poor devils?

27 March

Revolution in Yugoslavia.

29 March

Mum treated me to the flicks at the Rivoli—not bad.

1 April

Beware April 1st! Shoes soled 4/-. New fountain pen 1/10d, new hat 10/6d, two shirts 17/6d, two pairs of socks 4/6d, two pants 5/3d.

Sunday, 6 April

Germany attacked Greece and Yugoslavia. Mum and Dad went to Redhill to see Ida. I heard on the wireless the voice of a man who had been buried for eight days under a bombed Glasgow tenement.

10 April

Ida came up to see us.

Good Friday, 11 April

Given a day off!

15 April

Bought Rosa Knight a wedding present: a set of fruit bowls, Jones and Higgins, 5/9d. [*Rosa was 21 and lived in Peckham.*]

16 April

Afternoon off, went to pictures with Mum. Worst night raid we have had yet, 21:00 until 05:00.

17 April

I received telephone call for Selkirk, who had not then arrived, and was thus informed that there were 14,000 people in rest centres in London. I had to reply that Camberwell took 2,000 people into centres last night and could not take any from other boroughs. We cannot possibly cope today. Many families will have to stay in the schools for a while. We dealt with a tiny minority. Talfourd Road had been flattened and there had been parachute mines exploding all over the place, including Shardeloes Road, Brockley.

18 April

Re-housed many more.

19 April

Re-housed many more. Some are so grateful that it brings tears to the eyes. Late evening wrote to Ida, for her birthday, enclosing a 5/- postal order that Mum had bought for me during the day. Very heavy blitz at night, 21:30 until 05:00.

Sunday, 20 April

All centres are full. I worked hard all day re-housing the homeless, had no lunch, only endless cups of tea. God Bless the W.V.S. Selkirk is thankful that I did not let on that he was missing the other morning. He told me confidentially that the total now in centres in London was 28,000.

21 April

No raid last night, thank God. Dealt with very large numbers of people today, working 09:00 to 18:30. Am exhausted.

22–25 April

Same hours each day. Re-housed many families. Selkirk says that I really must have Saturday off. He will expect me in on Sunday, refreshed! Pompous ass.

27–29 April

Hours same. Re-housed many.

30 April

Rosa's last day. I drank her health at work (in port), also I went out to lunch with her and 'Tommy' Thompson (health visitor). We gave her our presents. I shan't marry until after the war, it is too hard for the widows.

1 May

Lunch out—1/11d; then I gave 2d to a plausible tramp (army deserter?—poor sod—he will get caught).

Sunday, 4 May

Day off, at last I did some librarianship study.

7 May

On all day, then fire duty 07:00–21:00.

8 May

On all day 09:00 to 17:00. Then fire watch 17:00–09:00. Twenty-three German planes shot down during the night, we are beginning to win now! So hungry after fire watch that I went out and spent 3/2d on unrationed food nearby and ate the lot!

9 May

We lost 10 planes over Germany last night, highest yet, but we shot down 13. They will soon call on me.

10 May

On 09:00–17:00. Rosa's wedding. Saturday night was an awful raid with damage to the Houses of Parliament, Westminster Hall, the Abbey, Old Kent Road, Peckham Road and one bomb landed outside our office (A.E.U.). Luckily the firewatcher had left the roof for a moment, otherwise the blast would have done for him. I am duty firewatcher tomorrow night. No phones now, no water, lovely big tree down. The library ruin now totally demolished by another high explosive bomb. (They often fall on buildings already hit). We shot down 33 planes.

Sunday, 11 May

I should have gone to work for 09:00. Mum could not wake me (she says). I slept all day! Got to work for fire-watching at 17:00 walking the last part of the way. Sherwood said

Selkirk assumed that I was as he quaintly put it 'a morbid statistic'.

Noisy night, on alone as second person on rota, Wilkins, did not turn up. I'm not afraid, but better with two people as building very large.

12 May

On 09:00–17:30 after fire-watching. A very busy day. Last night's bombs were nearer than I knew at the time. Hatcham Road, Peckham Road, Wells Way, Warner Road, Denmark Road, Lowth Road and Grummant Road.

13 May

A letter from Auntie. Awfully busy again and long roundabout walks to and from work. Brockley, Nunhead, Peckham, Camberwell. No trams, an enormous crater outside the office.

14–20 May

No lunch again today. Home by 19:00. Re-housed hundreds.

Each day is similar, getting to work by 09:00 and home by 19:00 and re-housing large numbers.

21 May

Wonderful Auntie sent me a good luck card by first post. To Croydon Polytechnic to take the Elementary Examination of the Library Association. Selkirk gave me the day off and is the only person there who does not think I'm barmy doing this. The other nine candidates were all girls, so I was glad to be wearing both the A.R.P. and the Royal Air Force Reserve badges.

22 May

Both Selkirk and Miss Ryder are very interested in my literature exam paper. I paid 6d for a share in a raffle for a 15/- savings certificate. Received the latest issue of the Camberwell staff magazine *All's Well*, which gets dirtier.

25 May

I am now working 09:00–18:00 every day including Sundays. I do all the Ministry Returns and the Key and Property Indexes, working in lulls. I would rather study, but they rely on me to do them.

28 May

My 19th birthday. *O tempora, o mores!* Auntie sent me £1/1 cheque with a card and a nice encouraging letter. Mum and Dad each gave me 5/-. I took time off at what should be lunchtime and walked to Rye Lane and bought a loose-leaf notebook.

31 May

A half-day, so went to pictures with Mum. Saw Margaret Lockwood *Quiet Wedding*, excellent, plus *Hopalong Cassidy* second film, which Mum did not like.

Sunday, 1 June

Day off! Went on solitary walk Box Hill etc, not bad walked miles and got very stiff for lack of practice, all for 4/-.

2 June

Bank holiday. On duty 09:00 until 18:00. Very busy then walked over to the Town Hall for fire-watch 18:00 until 21:00. Good to fire-watch here as breakfast is provided, egg, bacon and fried bread then straight back to work at A.E.U. building. Dozed off once or twice and Sherwood said I must have been on the tiles last night. He's quite a funny old sod really.

4 June

A lull in the bombing with me getting up to date with the Ministry figures. Lunch at Queens, excellent but expensive at 2/1d.

Sunday, 8 June

A day off. Read Edgar Wallace *A Debt Discharged*.

10 June

Reading *By Force of Circumstance* by Lewis Tracy, it's a mystery. Haircut 1/- (wartime inflation).

12 June

On 09:00–17:00. In evening heard *Life of Ben Jonson* on wireless. Today I received a bill for 1/5d for the breakfast I had at the Town Hall when I did the last fire-watch. There was a note appended: 'In future you will be paid 3/- for each fire-watch duty at the Town Hall.'

13 Friday

After work, chanced my luck with bombs and went to flicks, *Philadelphia Story*, Katharine Hepburn, bad luck restricted to that.

16 and 17 June

Lovely weather. Work 9:00–17:30.

18 June

Same duty. Sherwood off to have his ulcerated leg stump attended to, he is a stoical sufferer.

19 June

Selkirk gave me a Penguin, *European Painting and Sculpture* and then said that the Ministry wanted the statistics reworked to show re-housed adults and children separately for each quarter and I would be the best person to do it. Bought five razor blades 1/3d.

Sunday, 22 June

Sunbathed in garden, very warm.

23–25 June

09:00–18:00 each day. New glasses, £1/7/6.

26 June

09:00–17:00. Then 17:00–09:00, fire-watching at Art Gallery with Selkirk Chapman. A short air raid alert. Nothing. Discussion all rest of night on European painting, mostly a monologue from him as I had not read the book very closely, interesting. Straight on to work.

Friday, 27 June

09:00–17:00. Lunchtime opened a bank account at Barclays.

Saturday, 28 June

I was given a half-day. I bought two vests at Kerry's, Brockley Cross. Cinema in evening.

Sunday, 29 June

Day off.

2 July

Half-day. Went with Dad to Norbury [*Emm's house*] in afternoon by two trams. Garden is overgrown, but the usual lovely flowers. Picked a bunch for Mother. We worked at the garden.

3 July

09:00–17:30. A.E.U. fire-watch (now 22:00–09:00 which is much better).

4 and 5 July

09:00–17:00. Ida and Mac over for a week's stay.

10 July

I went to meet the district valuer at Norbury at 11:00, difficult to arrange as Sherwood off to Roehampton re leg-stump ulcers and Boyle wangled half-day for her complicated social life. Valuer OK. Wrote to Auntie.

11 July

On 09:00–18:00. Very hot.

12 July

09:00–18:00. At lunchtime I had to go to the Labour Exchange to answer a demand that I register for military service. Clerks stupid, and it took some time to get them to note down my R.A.F. Volunteer Reserve number and check it. They knew that I had had an eye test. Night on fire-watch at Wilson's.

Sunday, 13 July

Off.

14 July

Letter from Auntie with £1 for my new bank account. She is a dear.

15 July

Doug to supper to arrange a week's walking holiday.

19 July

Fire-watch at the art gallery 17:00–09:00, back to old time. On alone, went off to sleep at table by the telephone.

20 Sunday

Off at 09:00. Home as soon as possible, Doug was waiting, so soon we were off to Reading by coach from Victoria. We then walked to Bucklebury Youth Hostel for the night. Monday to Henley. Rest of the holiday walks to Speen, Jordans, Chesham, Hemel Hempstead, Speen again, Boulters Lock. Home then, as too wet to go on. Total cost: £4/19/5. Had bath and washed hair. Wrote to Auntie. Night raid 02:00–04:00, but stayed upstairs. Burbage Road hit, Herne Hill.

28 July

Back to work. 09:00–17:00 all week.

1 August

09:00–17:00. Mum collected holiday snaps, Co-op (total cost with films 14/3d). Fire watch at Art Gallery, 17:00–09:00.

4 August

Bank holiday Monday. My first one off for years.

5 and 6 August

09:00–17:30. Notification that I passed the Library Association Entrance Examination.

7 and 8 August

09:00–17:30. Busy dealing with families returning from evacuation in country and finding their homes bombed and uninhabitable.

9 August

Half-day. I bought shoes and *The Century's Poetry, 1837–1937* 2 vols. 1/-.

Sunday, 10 August

On 09:00–17:00. Only Selkirk and Betty Davis turned up. They can't all be dead! No raid.

13 August

Took Grandad back his First Aid book, which he asked Mum for. Can't think he will use it.

14 August

I was given a half-day off. Mum treated me to the Rivoli, Shaw's *Major Barbara*. We were both very impressed. Wrote to Auntie.

15 and 16 August

On 09:00–17:35. Collected my watch from Tuppenham's, repaired for 5/-. I am reading a stodgy biography of *J.M. Barrie* by Dennis Mackail.

Sunday 17 August

Given day off.

18 August

Busy. 4,106 persons re-housed last quarter.

19 August

Lunch with Mrs Boyle at the emergency feeding centre for 10d. I find it odd that such a 'refined' person would eat in such a place without the necessity to do so. It will be my one and only visit, an experience of fish soup, national bread and strong tea.

20–27 August

Hours each day 09:00–17:30 with one night fire-watching at Wilson's Grammar School until 09:00 next morning.

28 August

A half-day. Bought an ever-ready torch for 3/- and H.M.V. all-wave radio for £8/8 including £2 out of Mum's housekeeping money. All previous wireless sets have been homemade or second-hand ones repaired by me.

Sunday, 31 August

A day off. I helped Mum get rid of soot and plaster dust upstairs. The window holes have thin cotton sheets nailed over them and the rain drives in. Listened to *The Brains Trust* on new wireless and read.

1 September

09:00–17:00 this week.

3 September

I stayed all night on fire-watch with Selkirk Chapman who has now been directed to add his own name to the rota. He brought along J.S. Whales *Christian Doctrine*, which he used as the basis of an all-night discussion with me.

4 September

I received a National Service registration card with my age shown as 39, no wonder I'm not in the R.A.F. yet as they think I'm already too old! Sent it back corrected. Wrote to Auntie. Now hours are 09:00–17:30 each day.

12 September

In evening I treated Mum to the New Cross Kinema, we saw Leslie Banks and Alistair Sim in *Cottage to Let*.

13 September

On 09:00–17:00, then fire-watching at the Art Gallery, 17:00–21:00. Another building to get to know. Uncle John had art courses here, I believe.

Sunday, 14 September

Went to tea at Selkirk Chapman's flat, 14, Howard Court, Peckham Rye, to listen to some of his records. The block of flats was newly completed just as the war began. He is a very cultivated, effeminate Cambridge graduate from Stockport. He knew nobody in the London area. He is relaxed in my company, which intrigues me as he is in his late 30's. Music is his great love and we listened to classical recordings and drank excellent coffee, which he manages to have available. The recordings, which he asserted were the best, included Liszt concertos, Debussy, Franck, 'Symphonic Variations', followed by his enlightening me about the structure and merits of each.

16 September

I received a corrected National Service card, so I shall soon be in the R.A.F.. Read *In the Mill* John Masefield.

24 September

I started Wednesday afternoon classes at Brixton. Selkirk can't guarantee that I won't be on duty sometimes and have to miss them.

25 September

On 09:00–17:00, and then fire-watching at Wilson's Grammar School all night. I now visit Selkirk one evening a week from 19:30 to around 22:30. We discuss literature and politics endlessly and I have to develop at great length any argument I put forward, so it is highly educational.

27 September

A further medical examination for the Air Force. I hope they are not trying to reject me on eyesight.

30 September

R.A.F. medical was OK except that they will not pass me until I have visited one of their eye specialists.

2 October

I had an appointment at 09:30 with a Dr Finlay at Charlton. He arrived at 11:30. Lots of irritating eye tests, but a nice friendly talk about what I was doing and what I would like to do. He passed me for R.A.F. ground crew. Good. Wrote to Auntie. Fire-watch in evening at Art Gallery. Read Jeavon's *Principles of Science*.

8 October

In afternoon to Brixton librarianship classes.

9 October

On 09:00–17:35. In the evening lacquered Mum's large black metal tray. Did some study. Have been sleeping in my bedroom for some time now, it's very cold without a window, but now only the noise of trains and trams.

11 October

I worked from 09:00–12:00. Treated Mum to Odeon at Deptford. *Lady Hamilton* which we both thought excellent. I paid Weech and Co. 13/6d for repairing our mains unit for the wireless.

12 October

I am teaching Miss Davis my work. We all expect me to be called any day now. Wrote to Auntie.

13 October

A half-day. Attended librarianship classes at Brixton. Heard from Auntie at last; she is far from well.

14 October

A day off as I did not have any holiday in the summer. Did some study. Then 17:00 fire-watch at the A.E.U. with Weatherall, who I have not seen for ages. He failed his medical but is a pacifist anyway, and they have left him on library work for the present.

24 October

09:00–17:30 then on to 21 Camberwell Grove for a good housewarming party for Miss Tabor (Tabby) and Miss Hamilton (Tweedy—she does not know her nickname). Saw Phyllis Pearson home and made a date. She works in the re-housing office.

26 October

Off for holiday time owing to me.

27 October

Able to get Auntie a jelly. Fire-watch A.E.U. 17:50–09:00.

28 October

Another day off for past holidays given up. To Norbury to see the surveyor about weatherproofing repairs. In evening took Phyllis to Lewisham Gaumont.

30 October

Wrote to Auntie. On 09:00–17:15. Went to Selkirk Chapman's 19:30 to hear *Symphonie Fantastique* six records, excellent.

31 October

At work 9:00–17:00. Then fire-watch at Town Hall with Mr Leonard, a sanitary inspector. Played chess all night, he won.

Sunday, 2 November

Off studying.

8 November

With Phil to the Gaumont Haymarket to see *Citizen Kane*, 4/6d each. Then Strand Corner House for tea. Then 12 bus to King's Arms, Peckham Rye. Walked and cuddled.

10 November

In evening to Selkirk's for music (Bach chorales) and coffee.

11 November

A letter from Bunny (Brenda Halls). Meet?

14 November

Date with Phil from work. Queen's Cafe for tea then Gaumont Lewisham, back to her home for supper.

15 November

Worked 09:00–17:00. Ida and Mac up for weekend.

16 November

Phil to tea. I've got very fond of her. We spend three evenings a week together. We exchange visits to our homes for Sunday tea and go on rambles around Sevenoaks and Keston, (and we do not walk all the time.) Doug Latham is quite displaced. Phil obtained a permit for the wool and is knitting me blue Air Force gloves as I am in the Royal Air Force Volunteer Reserve awaiting the day. At home, the fire is lit in the front room just for us and we look at my books etc. We often go to the cinema at the Odeon, Goose Green, Capitol, Forest Hill, Odeon, Peckham, and Tower, Rye Lane, seeing such classics as *When Ladies Meet* (Robert Taylor), *Penn of Pennsylvania*, *Sullivan's Travels*, *Lydia*, and Greta Garbo in *Two-Faced Woman*.

Sometimes we go to the West End to the Empire, Leicester Square and follow on with a meal at the Strand Corner House. We also saw Priestley's skit on the BBC. *Goodnight Children* at the New Theatre a 15/- matinee, then on to a newsreel theatre for a cuddle. I always pay and always walk her home to Lanbury Road, Peckham Rye, by around 23:00, half an hour after the time she is expected to get in.

On occasion I still take Mother to the cinema and we saw *Hellzapoppin'* around this time. Phil has a brother who is a pilot in the Fleet Air Arm. He has a pretty girlfriend and I am sure that his mother lives in fear that he might be killed; not unreasonable in the circumstances.

At the office Phil and I were for a time so successful in hiding our relationship that one day I was sent for by the supervisor, Miss Hamilton, a tweedy upper-middle-class Scot, and told that Betty Davis would have to be moved to other work as I was clearly spending time flirting with her. The amazing thing is that she was a library assistant, engaged to a chap in the Army and just fun to work with. I expect she will laugh her way through the whole war; I hope so. I didn't fancy her, just know her well from working together previously in Dulwich Library. I was able with some confidence to scotch that one and Betty was not moved.

17 November

To Selkirk's in evening for music, 19:30–22:00.

18 November

My dear Auntie Emm died at Carlisle at 05:00 (the telegram came before I left for work).

19 November

09:00–13:30. then on to librarianship course at Brixton.

20 November

I wrote to Uncle John and Auntie Kate, Mrs Leslie, etc. Fire watch at Wilson's School at 17:00.

22 November

Met Mum at New Cross Gate photographers (before I go).

John in uniform.

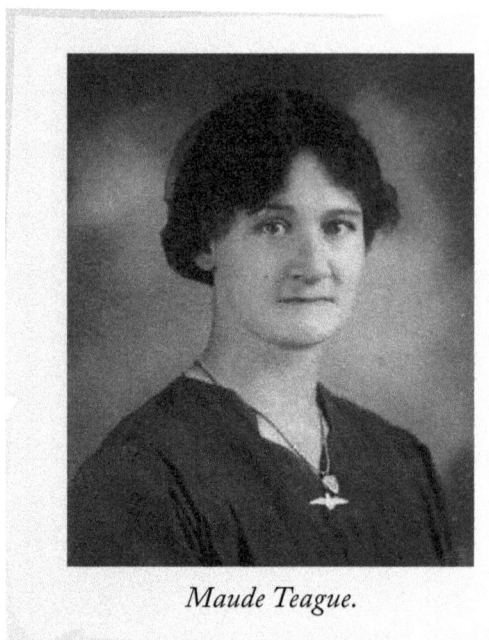
Maude Teague.

23 November

Tea with Phil at 16:00.

24 November

Working 09:00–17:00. To Selkirk's for evening. Tchaikovsky, 4th Symphony, excellent. Mum gave me a tin of milk for him. He was excessively grateful.

25 November

Pen repaired for 3/4d. Dear Auntie had to be buried at Holme Eden because of the war. Uncle John is one of the executors.

26 November

Afternoon classes at Brixton.

27 November

Selkirk has to do a survey of air raid shelters in the borough and he has passed it on to me. It involves going around in a stretcher car with a list, checking shelters are still extant.

29 November

Working 09:00–12:00. In afternoon took Phil to see *Hatter's Castle*, excellent. Then tea at Lyons Corner House. Miss Burton saw us there—it will come out now. Total cost 11/11d.

Sunday, 30 November

Dad's birthday. I bought him a new fountain pen. Mum paid half.

3 December

Half-day, to class at Brixton.

5 December

09:00–17:00, then took Phil to Odeon, Goose Green, saw *49th. Parallel*, then tea at East Dulwich, then home to her house for supper.

8 December

Working 09:00–17:00. To Chapman's 19:30–22:00. Music was good. Coffee in his Harrod's crockery. He fusses round in his kitchenette making it like an old hen.

9 December

I bought Mum gloves for Christmas early in case I'm elsewhere. Bought 1/6d concert ticket to help Russia but will not attend.

11 December

09:00–17:00 then fire watch at the Art Gallery until 09:00. A very, very cold night. I hope I don't get chilblains.

13 December

On 09:00–12:00, then home with Phil for lunch, then to the Gaumont, Haymarket to see *Sundown*. Tea at the Strand Corner House.

14 December

Phil to tea. Mum gave her two handmade handkerchiefs.

17 December

Half-day then classes at Brixton.

18 December

Auntie's birthday.

19 December

I posted card and book token to Phil for Christmas.

Sunday, 21 December

To Phil's for tea. She gave me a silver pencil for Christmas. Home before 23:00.

22 December

To Selkirk's for the evening. He gave me three-quarters of a pound of granulated sugar for Christmas. He got all huffy when I joked that he must have got it illegally. Mum says I'm tactless and shouldn't look a gift horse in the mouth.

Christmas Day, 25 December

My day off. Listened to the King's speech on the wireless.

26 December

At work 09:00–17:00. Took cold pork sandwiches for lunch, lovely. 19:00 to Phil for evening walk.

29 December

09:00–12:00 Then to Stoll Kingsway with Phil sat in Grand Circle. Nervo and Knox in *Babes in the Wood*, excellent. Tea in the Corner House. Home at 22:30.

1942

1 January

'*Dulce et decorum est pro patria mori*'—Oh Yes, of course!

'Civilization is a race between education and catastrophe.' H.G. Wells

9 January

I received 'the King's shilling', literally, at Padgate Air Base, near Warrington, Lancs.

Air Raids and RAF Days

Padgate

January and February

At the outset I signed over to Mother a shilling a day of my pay so that she would get a small pension if I was killed. My parents and I exchange letters at least twice a week and they always post to me *The New Statesman* and *The Observer*. Mother does my washing and starches my shirt collars. Yes we do wear black ties on Air Force blue shirts with attached collars and the tunic is like the jacket of a suit.

I usually put chocolate and cigarettes in my parcel of dirty washing as we have special rations of these. The clean laundry that Mother sends back always includes a chocolate Swiss roll, sometimes two, so I am never short of friends, as, living in the open air in all weathers, we are always hungry. The parcels are in brown paper and string of course, which we re-use to destruction.

Phil and I exchanged letters of undying love several times a week for a while, but lately they have become less frequent.

I attend the nearest Methodist Church except when on church parade, when I have learned to be C. of E. for speed. The 'odds & sods' are often kept waiting until the C. of E. are marched off.

March to July

Next, I was posted to Blackpool where boarding houses are used as billets, with catering provided by the landladies who are allocated special rations. I was sent to 81, Topping Street, then later to 39, Hull Road.

Physical training was done on the sands, Morse training was in the concourse of one of the railway stations. Rifle-firing and grenade throwing was on one area of beach. The Imperial Hotel was the H.Q. of 2 Wing.

Whilst at Blackpool I enjoyed some good music, for there was an R.A.F. Music Society that met at the grammar school for listening to records. There we enjoyed Beethoven, Brahms, Purcell and Tchaikovsky. Some live concerts were held there, such as a Polish airman playing Chopin. At other times we had pianist, Myers Foggin, also in the R.A.F. and Arthur Catterall. Sometimes there was a symphony concert in the Tower Ballroom and I and my friends usually followed the music up with a supper at the Methodist Church Hall. There was an R.A.F. Lending Library too.

Blackpool after three weeks in the Air Force. John is in the second row, second from the right.

I made particular friends with Harry Strong, a schoolmaster from Chertsey, Guy Worsdell, a birthright Quaker from Gloucester and Ron Speed. We all discussed politics, books and music and played chess and table tennis and went putting in Stanley Park. When we were both free, Guy and I sometimes took the tram to Squires Gate and had a lovely walk across the sands to St Anne's. On other occasions, we paid 4d for the tram to Fleetwood, took the ferry and had a country walk.

Part of short leaves was spent with Phil, and we saw *Tomorrow Will Dawn* at the Odeon. I began to be convinced that I should not become seriously involved until after the war.

Guy and I saw John Gielgud in *Macbeth* for 2/- special rate in Manchester and also went to a Halle concert. I saw Robert Newton and Mary Clare in *No Orchids for Miss Blandish* at the Blackpool Grand, *Wings of the Morning* (Leslie Banks), *The Great Lie* (Bette Davis) and *One of Our Aircraft is Missing*. I read William Shirer *Berlin Diary*.

I purchased a map of the Lake District for 4/- and in June obtained a pass for Carnforth and Guy and I spent a lovely day at Arnside, Silverdale and Carnforth. We enjoyed beautiful views across the Kent Estuary.

I found Guy excellent company, although he was a misogynist and carped on not getting involved with women, because they'd be sure to hinder developing one's full potential in life. At the same time I assessed that he was totally without ambition; he even suggested that my intention to work at becoming a qualified librarian in spite of the Air Force was 'bourgeois'. Guy, I now know was a Quaker only in demeanour. Years later there was a girl and he told me she made all the running, but I don't know if they married.

As to Brockley at this time, the front gate and railings were taken for salvage to make shells and a tram was derailed at Brockley Cross with one killed and six injured.

16 July

Phyllis told me that she was sure that I did not love her in a committed way and believed she felt less keen on me, so we must not get passionate. I confided in my parents who were understanding.

It was a very sad leave because my second-best school friend, Caswallon Evans, committed suicide in the gas oven at his home. He was 19 and a civil service clerk.

Dad was on night duty but treated Mum and I to the cinema to see, *How Green Was My Valley* and Mother provided a marvellous supper together before he went on duty. They used to save up their food points for these occasions.

I wrote my first will. I had not bothered during the bombing, but I had still only a minuscule amount saved.

Then back to Blackpool for the bullshit of passing out parade before the Air Minister, Archibald Sinclair. I was on his guard of honour, which involved much drilling in advance. I was also on 24-hour guard at the H.Q., the Imperial Hotel, actually standing on guard for a total of seven hours.

There were also training sessions on the assault course and firing ranges and route marches, one in full-kit to Rossall and back. The worst was a forced route march in full-kit, all of the 16 miles to Rea Green. I grimly kept up where I started near the front rank and I had one of Mother's Swiss rolls packed away somewhere and shared it with friends and we drank one pint of shandy each. I had three very large blisters which Ken, who desperately wanted to be a doctor, dealt with using a bloody great darning needle. We all stayed in that evening stretched out on our beds.

My next posting was to Yatesbury, Wiltshire. I do love the country here. The camp nestles among the hilltops, providing a prevailing westerly breeze and the beauty of the changing colours of the hills. I wish my dear parents could enjoy this countryside.

I often walked with amenable friends over the hills to Devizes, on to Melksham for lunch, on to Chippenham for tea then hitching lifts in service lorries back to Yatesbury.

At each place we ate very well at church halls where nice ladies thought we needed feeding to country standards. We were stuffed with eggs, bacon, beautiful ham, jam, cakes and milk. On Sunday evenings, I often walked to a church with an appropriate companion and even sampled Christian Science in Swindon—not a bad service.

Sometimes I did my study reading or wrote letters on my own sitting just under the White Horse. I was working on Library Association correspondence courses with Walford, Corbett and Phillips as tutors.

19 August

Food is worse than ever. Raid on Dieppe by land, sea and air forces, Canadian and British. I was on guard at the camp hospital—an airman patient gone mad, poor sod.

27 August

Air raid warning just as enemy planes appeared over the horizon with shells from the A.A. guns bursting all around them. I passed my technical test with full marks, now on to Receiver 1082 and Transmitter 1083.

September

Low marks for the first lesson of my librarianship correspondence course, written on knees sitting under a haystack. Pillow slips from home, lovely on these bloody straw pillows.

The next weekend at home, I took Mum to see Emlyn Williams in *The Morning Star*, a very well-acted play about the London Blitz, 12/6d seats. On the Sunday Grandad Homewood and Mrs Green came to share our excellent lunch. In the afternoon I listened to Thomas Hardy, *Far From the Madding Crowd* on the radio and then had an excellent tea. Mum and Dad bothered to come with me to Paddington to see me off. We are really good companions.

27 September

Walked to Devizes; best views ever, dinner there, then walked over the hills to Bishops Canning—boiled eggs, bread and butter, jam and cream plus homemade cake.

28 September

I do not know how I could carry on without the marvellous food parcels my dear Mother sends me.

11 October

Guy and I walked 21 miles, Yatesbury to Calne, on to Chippenham for lunch then Keynton Langley and Castle Combe (said to be the prettiest village in England).

20 October

I purchased *The McColvin Report* (on post-war public library development) and was detailed for potato picking for a whole day.

24 October

We did a hilly cross-country run in the rain, (exhilarating) and attended a lecture by the Archbishop of Canterbury who unwittingly brought the house down when he said, 'One doesn't look at the clock on the mantelpiece when one is poking the fire.' (Temple was a lovely man, a real Archbishop, I believe).

21 St Norbert Rd
Brockley
SE4
24 October 1942

Dear John,

Just a few lines in reply to your letter we received this morning. I shall not post till Friday evening as it will not go out till then. I am very pleased to hear that you have had a reply from Mr Phillips and note that he will deal with your correspondence course while he is able. Sorry to hear that you have had a nasty head cold; perhaps it was due to you having your locks shorn. Also, I am pleased to hear that you passed the Morse with an 'A'.

Mum has mentioned in her letter to you that I had received another letter from Uncle John enclosing a cheque, which I have acknowledged. You will be able to see the letter and my reply when next you are home here. He has sold [Emm's] house for £850. I cannot let you know fully by letter. It was a pity I did not receive it last week when you would have been able to see same.

He seems to have done fairly well with regards to house as we agreed to take £700 minimum but you will be able to pass your opinion when you have read the letter. It has been very muggy and mild here with very heavy rains and I think it has given me a slight return of lumbago. Must close now. But otherwise, I am feeling all right. I have to get myself ready to go on duty.

With all our best wishes and much love from us both.

God bless

Dad

November

I was awarded my 'sparks' and was very sorry that Harry Strong failed. We went out for the day to ease his great depression. We all wanted to stay together. We walked and hitched to Marlborough where we had an excellent lunch in a hotel, suffering disapproving glances, being the only non-commissioned chaps there. We then got a lift from one of these Army officers the 16 miles to Devizes, where we had a cream cake tea, then a lift from a farmer to Bockhampton, where we chatted up two W.A.A.F.s and had a brief kissing session before getting back to Yatesbury.

Another marathon outing involved walking with Guy to Marlborough for an excellent lunch, then in the afternoon walking on to Savernake Forest and back to Yatesbury. We had two teas, one excellent and one at the Y.M.C.A. The food at Yatesbury is very bad.

18 November

The anniversary of dear Auntie's death. Sent money and a card for flowers for her grave. I plan to do this every year.

(But my ideas changed about cemeteries, and I never did).

A few weeks elapsed between completing my training and being posted.

I was not best pleased as I was sent to an overseas posting unit (with my friend Ron Speed, just the two of us). It was Wilmslow in Cheshire. Promptly, I had a studio photograph taken and sent home in case the end was near. Dad hurriedly bought me the signet ring I lusted for as my 21st birthday present, six months in advance.

I was issued with a First World War rifle and put on guard duty. I had fired such a rifle twice, but would have been pretty useless at that stage, even though I felt I should be a real guard at that camp whereas guarding a Blackpool Hotel had seemed somehow unreal. Ron Speed was issued with Iceland gear.

After TWO DAYS I was posted to Castle Kennedy near Stranraer, Wigtownshire, Scotland. It was an operational signals unit still being developed on a deeply wooded estate. There was no railway station, just a halt and as it was pitch dark when I got there and the train was unlit and I could not see. I stepped out of the door in full kit with my kit bag laid across the top of my large back pack by a kind squaddie on the train, and I plunged into space and down the railway embankment arse over tip. Providentially I was more or less unhurt but totally shocked and blasphemous (I was getting practised by then).

I dumped my stuff and found that there was a truck awaiting me in the nearby lane. I was allocated to a wooden barrack hut among the trees and late the next day I unpacked receivers and transmitters and helped to set them up in one of these huts and was soon receiving Morse-coded signals from the Air Ministry and responding. I was very green at it and I am sure there were lots of garbled messages, but as these were in secret codes quite apart from the Morse, I never knew. We never discovered why telephones, suitably safeguarded were not used within the United Kingdom.

Of course there would be many exchange links to take care of. When not duty signals operator I was free, free to saw trees and chop wood and make a wooden hut warm and comfortable. Twice when I had achieved this I was ordered to move on to another hut and start all over again.

So I learned that it was best just to vanish when not on duty and walk to Stranraer, or Dumfries. Thus I saw films such as *Reap the Wild Wind* and *Ships with Wings* (Leslie Banks). I did get put on two charges there, one for vanishing when I was on standby. At this time the French Navy scuttled itself.

Ida and Alvin had furnished lodgings in Haywards Heath; they stayed at Brockley now and then, together with Ida's dog and once or twice I had leave partly overlapping.

Ida

December

My cousin Jack Teague was serving in the Air Force on St. Mary's Scilly Islands, and remained there a very long time. He was probably on radar detectors.

One delight at Stranraer was fitting up a field telephone link from the entrance gate to H.Q. I had to fix wires up telegraph poles; I was terrified but had to do it; thank goodness it worked and that was that. Then the wing commander inspected and noticed an aerial on the roof of the house and I was one of the Erks commanded to 'take the bloody thing down and put it somewhere less conspicuous.' Luckily there was a trapdoor onto the roof.

Next, I had to learn to operate a 56-line switchboard and soon I was on another charge for saying 'Right-oh' to the station commander when he asked me to get him a number.

Food was very poor on this R.A.F. station and I stuffed myself on excellent meals in church halls in Stranraer.

I bought Priestley's autobiography, *Rain Upon Godshill*, to add to my collection and read this in one night on duty. That same evening, I tried to ring Mrs Jeavons next door to Mother but was caught by the local exchange woman being suspicious of the manner in which I asked her to do it. This time the duty officer shouted at me to try not to be such a bloody fool.

As a matter of fact, he said, I was posted to Anglesey, but could have Christmas leave first, so he was not such a bad sod. I even got my kit taken to the railway halt and the train stopped when I waved it down. Two days later I was at Joanne's, New Cross, buying *The Beveridge Report* on the brave new world we were to set up when the war was over, and was very happy to be able to discover and buy a jar of pickled walnuts for our Christmas feast.

That winter we, that is, Mum, Dad and I went to West End Theatres, as and when we were free and together. Among other plays we saw: *The Man Who Came to Dinner*, at the Savoy, Michael Redgrave and Leslie Banks in *The Duke in Darkness* at the St James Theatre and *The Doctor's Dilemma* at the Haymarket. I paid my share always.

1943

Somehow, nearly all of the 1943 diary got deleted from my computer disc, so most of what follows is a summary. [*John noted this in his 80's.*]

1 January

I reported to R.A.F. Mona, Anglesey, a Flying Training Command airfield almost exactly in the middle of the island. I was billeted in a Nissan hut under a clump of pine trees and in the first week, early one morning, I watched a mare give birth to a foal. She bit the cord. The baby scrambled up on its stick-like legs and leaned on the mare's legs and she moved away a little in order to make it stand on its own. It fell over, but scrambled up and staggered to its mother and began suckling.

21 St Norbert Rd
Brockley
1 January 1943

My dear son,

Your welcome letter arrived second post today. Hope you have received letter from me and parcel posted on the 30th. Dad has written two letters to you. I am sorry to hear that weather is so bad it snowed hard all night Tuesday and today it is raining, do take care of yourself and dry your clothes as soon as you can. Have you succeeded in taming your little mouse, Friday (the cat) would soon tame it. Fred seems to have a full-time job looking after you. He seems a very decent sort of boy.

I should like to see you all dressed up I bet you look funny. I hope you were able to drink our health we drank to you and your friends, Dad at the post and me by myself at home with pussycats.

Dad and I have been listening to the New Year Festival and Grand Pageant of the Empire and her allies. China got a very big cheer and so did the Navy and so did the Air Force.

Dad will answer your next letter he is sending you a platinum nib wrapped in some washing and hopes it will arrive safely. When I go to Jones again, I will try and order some more, it is rather a job there to order anything. I should think the mountains must look lovely on an early summer morning.

I have finished my book and enjoyed reading it.

With our fondest love to you dear boy.

God bless and protect you

your loving Mum and Dad xx

The card index of bomb-damaged housing at Lewisham Central Library records 18 January 1943 for 21 St Norbert Road 'badly damaged but habitable'. On that raid 30 houses were destroyed round the corner in Arica Road with 34 killed.

Our water was dark brown, from a lake across the road: it was raised up a water tower and fed straight into the pipes, untreated. The tea was awful! R.A.F. Mona adjoins the village of Gwalchmai, in a very Welsh part of Wales, totally Welsh speaking and very, very rural with no traffic except that of the armed services to Holyhead and R.A.F. Valley, together with a few farmers' cars, lorries and tractors and the odd bus.

I was thrown in at the deep end here, servicing on flight dispersal points, but I had little problem with that or with service life in general for I had found my feet by then and training had made me confident in checking aircraft radio. We were training pilots and there was plenty of flying and the usual complement of horrific crashes.

The nearest small town was Llangefni, a market town in the centre of Anglesey. Rapidly I discovered the hotel there and went for lunch or dinner in a large upstairs room, where I enjoyed generous helpings of roast ham, chicken, beef or lamb, with great quantities of fresh vegetables. The puddings were in large helpings, too, my favourite being apple pie with lashings of rich cream. Then there was coffee and I avoided the booze.

The places visited for cinemas were Bangor and Holyhead. Llanfair PG of course had to be visited at least once as did Snowdon.

May

I was posted to Wrexham, North Wales, but the signal must have been misread and I was sent to Wretham in Norfolk and managed to get the rail travel warrant made out via London. A very brief visit home, then on to Norfolk where R.A.F. Wretham had no knowledge of my posting to them. They decided (how?) that it was meant to be Waddon, so I was despatched there by lorry.

Both these East Anglian airfields were operational and the accommodation was in brick-built pre-war barrack blocks, small and humane and I should have liked to have been posted to either. R.A.F. Waddon, however sent a signal to the Air Ministry and discovered that I was posted to Wrexham, North Wales.

That same day they issued me with a rail warrant and I was driven by a W.A.A.F. in an R.A.F. car to some nameless East Anglian station.

Wrexham

At R.A.F. Wrexham I was posted 'absent without leave' and the explanation was cynically received and checked.

It was a Flying Training Command Unit and I had a brief but busy time there. Leisure trips were to Chester and Carnforth (for the Lake District) with cinema visits to Wrexham. Many hundreds of workers from Woolwich Arsenal had been transferred to a munitions factory at Wrexham and there were lots of lonely married women among them.

I was not averse to taking one of the younger of them to the cinema with a few kisses and cuddles and a few drinks thrown in, but I was shocked by being accosted and offered sex near the airfield by an 'oldish' woman with a cockney accent (in her thirties?). I said something to the effect that I was married and she said so was she and she was a bit contemptuous at my refusal.

I got to know the centre of Chester quite well and was intrigued by 'The Rows' and there were the city walls and the cathedral to explore. Additionally, there was boating available as well as several cinemas and forces canteens.

November

I applied to go on a conversion course from Wireless Operator to Wireless Operator/Mechanic (WOM) at Cranwell and was posted there soon afterwards. Cranwell was No. 1 R.A.F. Radio School and was still run as the major R.A.F. College with strict pre-war discipline; all ranks on courses being treated as inferior beings to be drilled and instructed to high precision. Tunic belts had to be blancoed and brass buttons and boots highly polished.

Training went right down to making one's own radio terminals from a block of solid copper. We marched between classrooms, billets, gymnasium, dining room etc to martial brass-band music on the Tannoy. Rare days off were spent in Grantham, Sleaford and most importantly in Lincoln.

R.A.F. Cranwell

1944 — Cranwell

My leave began at 18:00 hours, 30 December 1943, but although several of us waited until 21:00 the taxi we had ordered did not turn up, it was bitterly cold and we finally persuaded another taxi company to come for us at 21:30. This delay meant that I reached Kings Cross at 03:20, walked to the embankment and caught a tram home, bed at 07:30. The next day I was fit only to play cards.

1 January

I bought Kinglake's *Eothen* and Henry Fielding's *Joseph Andrews* at Joanne's, New Cross, on way to Kinema where I saw an awful film.

Sunday, 2 January

I chopped firewood for Mother and we had Grandad and Mrs Green to tea and spent a very enjoyable evening before I walked them home. Mrs G. says I'm a dear. I have stopped going to church.

3 January

We went to the West End where I intended to treat them to *For Whom the Bell Tolls*, a film at the Carlton Haymarket. We were unable to get in (pity I was in civilian clothes), so we went to the Leicester Square Theatre where we saw *The Nelson Touch*, a war film but not too bad, Dad not impressed.

4 January

I went to Nunhead Library and Camberwell Re-housing Office to meet old friends. In the afternoon I took Mum to the Regal in Old Kent Road to see *Robin Hood* (in colour) and *Warn That Man*, Mother did not like.

There was an air raid warning at 02:30 but we stayed in bed.

5 January

I sawed up half a tree for logs and then repaired a two-valve radio for one of Dad's fellow air raid wardens, then I painted the woodwork in Ida's old bedroom.

6 January

I left for Cranwell on the 16:00 from Kings Cross.

8 January

The course is moving on fast, I am still reading my copy of Fielding's *Joseph Andrews* and saw film, in the Y.M.C.A. (old Gordon Harker, etc.).

12 January

I received a Christmas card from Ida, the weather was icy cold and there was much bullshit to endure. I saw one excellent film there, *Petrified Forest* with Bette Davis and Leslie Howard. Croydon was bombed, including the Davis Theatre and Grants.

13 January

I had teeth filled, as the R.A.F. dentist said 'You must get your choppers in good order before going overseas.'

15 January

I had a weekend pass but fog rather spoilt it. I caught a train from Grantham at 17:36, which was really the 14:00 running late, but it did not arrive at Kings Cross until 22:30 and I caught the 23:28 from London Bridge and went to see Dad at his air raid wardens' post on night duty during the early hours. Mum told me that she had said she would get me to call in in R.A.F. uniform (not knowing that I would be hours and hours late), so Dad could show me off to his friends.

Next day I got up late and worked about the house and as thick fog persisted, I returned to Cranwell early, leaving Brockley at 16:00, Grantham 21:30 and last bus to Cranwell.

Syd and two friends in ARP uniform. Syd in centre.

20 January

There was an Exchange Parade and I was able to exchange old, much-darned socks and repaired underpants for new.

My address here is: Dorm Z5, Block 325, B Squadron, 3 Wing, No. 1 Radio School.

21 January

A much heavier raid on London than for some time, with Wickham Road hit. In spare time, I continued to write to Guy, Harry Strong (in India), Ida (in Canada), home (twice a week) and Jimmy Booker, to play chess and table tennis and to read *The Observer* and *The New Statesman* all through.

26 January

In spite of the cold winter weather we did physical training several times a week, wearing only shorts, Ugh! We also had terribly strenuous defence exercises.

29 January

There was an air raid on Millwall, Bexley, etc.

4 February

More heavy raids on London (the Krauts are getting desperate). I received a heavily censored letter from Ida written from Toronto on 27 January. [After the war I learned that it gave forbidden details of her voyage on the crowded *Queen Mary* converted as a troopship.]

5 February

'X' has stolen some pass forms from Orderly Room, I forged one for the weekend from 17:00, also a coupon for 1 lb of oranges. Parents pleased with this treat for Mother's birthday. Left 17:00 on Sunday, back in billet by 22:30.

The next day I put in for an official pass for the weekend. Then I was made class leader for organised games (I must be caught!). This enabled me to mark present the scroungers who had previously done the same for me.

12 February

Took taxi to Grantham. Then air raid 21:07 whilst I was at London Bridge, one kite, heavy ack-ack overhead, I did my 'don't worry' act. Dad on at 22:00.

13 February

I commenced repainting the woodwork in my bedroom cream, but left for Cranwell at 18:00. There was a heavy raid on London that night, six aircraft shot down.

I continued to be class leader, covering for the scroungers from organised games, not playing myself as I was recording attendances.

17 February

Went to international show at Y.M.C.A., not bad, with a good French actress with a smashing figure. The next day I had an official ration of three oranges.

18 February

There was a raid on London. I had a dread feeling and got 'X' to sell me a blank pass. I forged it for Saturday and caught the 15:30 from Grantham, Kings Cross, 18:00, London Bridge 18:30 to New Cross Gate only (due to bombs), tram home from there. Parents OK.

Continued decoration of bedroom, ate lovely food. There were two raids that night, the first a heavy firebomb effort, but five planes were shot down.

19 February

The next day I visited Grandad, then home for pancakes (lovely), then caught 16:45 from Kings Cross.

22 February

Ten planes were shot down in a big raid on London.

23 February

Raids on London again.

24 February

13 planes shot down. I am re-reading my copy of *Natalie Maisie and Pavilastukay*, Masefield, there are many apt topical lines:

'When in his iron hat he trod his beats
Crunching at every step the fruits of strife
The powdered brick and glass that had been streets
And sad at the stupidity of life
Then like the lifting thrilling of a fife
Within his mind that City's image thrilled
Saying, 'much better things have once been willed'
Much better things, which can again be had will
Therefore, to possess the life you saw
Of men and women perfect, children glad
Living at peace in cities without flaw.'

25 February

'X' had no pass forms, so I went anyway without, even dodging recording attendance at organised games, arriving at Kings Cross in time to catch the 21:07 from London Bridge. Two raid-free nights. Spent in happiness.

However the train to Grantham was one hour late and I had to walk the 16 miles from Grantham to Cranwell in thick snow. 01:40 I chatted up the guard and slipped in with soaking wet feet. The next day I had a chronic pain in the groin, but it went by evening.

29 February

There was another raid on London, with two planes shot down.

3 March

I attended a concert in the Y.M.C.A., Beethoven's 8th and Schumann's 4th. That night there was a bomb on the railway behind our house (500 yards away) and a petrol bomb on a house in Finland Road. Nasty all round. All our window frames smashed out again. Letter from India,

Jimmy Booker's house has been bombed, I replied, also to his wife.

4 March

Home on forged pass. Mum was very shaken, Dad philosophical it missed! Food good. I continued to paint bedroom. Back on 17:00, base by 22:00.

8 March

London alert. Highly cheesed off with Cranwell.

10 March

An assault course where I could not reach the other side on ropes, a bloody nightmare. In the evening, I bought my chocolate ration to take home, having applied for a weekend pass. A Y.M.C.A. evening — Brahms, delightful!

11 March

Home legally, late at Kings Cross, 20.33 from London Bridge. Fine food, back on 17:00 from Kings Cross.

13 March

I worked on daily inspections of radios in Typhoons, interesting, Tuesday on Ansons.

17 March

More inoculations and vaccinations for foreign parts, worked on petrol generators with 'Beethoven Eroica Symphony' in the evening and there was a raid on London.

Sunday, 19 March

I was involved in a church parade with two march-pasts, silly bullshit. There was a night raid on Hull, but eight were downed.

21 March

The course reached the repair of radio sets, most satisfying. There were heavy raids on London on Tuesday and Wednesday nights. The vaccination this time went wrong with festering and I became ill but did not go sick. There was an examination of radio theory and I felt dreadful.

Worse on Saturday, when I reached home, unofficially, at 23:25, having to walk from New Cross. Dad dosed me heavily with whisky, Mum looked at the arm and threatened the doctor, so told her I was not officially on leave, which shook her. Unable to eat lovely meal, actually sick and feverish. On the Sunday I set off back dosed with whisky.

27 March

I reported sick in case arm was about to drop off. I did not get to the doctor, the W.A.A.F. orderly examined it and declared it normal.

1 April

As am better I slipped off to Grantham without a pass, by bus and train.

2 April

The forsythia and almond looked wonderful. I returned as usual without incident.

4 April

My name was listed as having passed the course.

5 April

I was given £1 ration money and told that I was to go on embarkation leave, destination unstated.

6 April

All leave was cancelled and we were put to digging additional defensive perimeter trenches (now I've done everything!).

7–11 April

Digging every day, with boozing trips to Lincoln each evening, totally shagged out. I went with a Will Waldron.

R.A.F. Driving School, Pwllheli, Wales

12 April

At 07:00 on I was posted immediately (without leave) to R.A.F. Driving School. Pwllheli, Wales. I was driven to Grantham at 08:00 and after eight changes of train arrived at 22:00 and billeted in a hotel, where there was nobody about, so I walked to the R.A.F. cookhouse and demanded food. A kindly W.A.A.F. duty cook fried me bacon, egg and chips, telling me it was an invasion training course including backing lorries up concrete ramps on the seafront.

Up at 07:00, checked in, inspected for pox and crabs etc. First driving lesson with pretty W.A.A.F. instructor in a large Ford V8 after a good lunch; they are in a hurry! Each evening cinema, each day driving to the peril of all and sundry, along impossible mountain lanes.

15 April

Have made friends with Jeff Jordan and went with him to Criccieth to meet two of his female friends who were starting a holiday there. We each paid half for tea at Black Beach (boiled eggs, cake etc.) and dinner at their hotel (three-course, chicken, excellent). In the afternoon, kissing and cuddling, then I went back and he stayed with the one he hopes to marry.

16 April

I went to Criccieth again to entertain the 'chaperone friend' we all had tea at The George and dinner at The Lion, a lovely sunny day. I sent Ida a cable for her birthday (2/6d).

18 April

Driving much improved.

19 April

Driving not so good.

20 April

I received a pullover from Mother, R.A.F. blue that she had knitted for me, enclosed was a letter stating that Uncle John was very ill.

Sunday, 22 April

I went to Portmadoc for tea, then to Borth Y Gest and back, with supper in Pwllheli.

23 April

I wrote to Aunt Kate and Uncle John who was on the danger list.

26 April

I was first on night driving, a beautiful night and the next day I was inoculated once more for overseas. I wrote to Guy, in Cheshire, and Harry Strong in India.

27 April

My first solo driving, appropriately I received a New Testament from Mrs Knapton that morning with an embarrassing letter about living in the light of Jesus.

John later added: *(Mrs Knapton was an elderly member of the Mothers Meeting at the Methodist Church. She was always dressed in black with a veil. She was a dear old soul.)*

Not having pranged I had high tea in Llanbedrog (two poached eggs, jam cake, tea). I walked each way with Jeff Jordan.

1 May

I drove for six hours and then wrote to Mrs Knapton thanking her for the N.T. and telling her I would carry it with me wherever I was in R.A.F. (I had Mother's Bible so far, but never more than glanced at it.) To the cinema in the evening with Jeff to see Bette Davis in *The Sisters*.

3 May

Solo night driving in convoy along mountain roads, bloody dark and no lights of course.

5 May

I was on the beer run to collect barrels from Llandudno where I had a good lunch at the Ritz Cafe. In evening saw *Kings Row* (a fine film) in Pwllheli.

Sunday, 7 May

A fine day, a late lie-in then explored local coastline alone, nobody else thought it worth the effort. Much enjoyed the beauty, bonus was an encounter with a trainee Wren officer who was reading poetry on a cliff. We both could spout Wordsworth and had a good kiss and cuddle as dusk fell and arranged to meet again.

8 May

I drove a three-ton Chev lorry in convoy at night.

9 May

I passed my driving test and board. To Beddgelert in evening saw Ralph Richardson in *Silver Fleet*, good.

10 May

I was posted to Halfpenny Green near Stourbridge in Worcestershire.

11 May

I explored Stourbridge, ate at the Conservative Club and went to the cinema.

12 May

I worked in the signals maintenance workshops, repairing sets. The next day I received wedding cake from Jimmy Booker.

Thereafter, I worked on B Flight in all weathers. Cinema included *Heaven Can Wait*, *The Life and Death of Colonel Blimp*, and the *Gang Show*.

16 May

Had a 24-hour pass, so I went to Birmingham via Stourbridge by bus. Good bed at Y.M.C.A. in High Street 1/- after seeing film *San Demetrio, London* at The Forum (excellent). Explored Brum. Matinee 3/- Birmingham Rep. *Six Characters in Search of an Author*. Bought Legouis *A Short History of English Literature*. I went to a news theatre in the evening before returning to Halfpenny Green.

Sunday, 21 May

Church parade with old-fashioned monarchist Canadian Padre (C. of E.), then duty in signals workshops, servicing generators. Bitterly cold. On Wednesday I went to Birmingham on a 24-hour pass to meet Guy, wearing shoes to shock him (he obeys rules). Stayed Y.M.C.A., he with local Quaker family. Saw two good films. On the Saturday I stayed in to see an ENSA show, *Without the Prince*, excellent acting.

Local pub crawl with Wooldridge, who lives in Stourbridge, one day; the next, alone to Sutton Coldfield where I walked in a marvellous park, returned last bus from Brum. On B Flight during day and on security patrol all one night, wet and unpleasant.

1 June

An Anson, I was going to service crashed in flames, crew all killed. I was upset and went boozing in the evening.

Inside an old Anson

5 June

Dad on holiday. Rome captured.

6 June

The invasion of Europe commenced in Normandy. Station cinema in evening *Action in the North Atlantic*.

8 June

I visited Brum alone, bought *The Poets and their Critics*, ate at Y.M.C.A. (good) and saw *Phantom of the Opera* (Technicolor), returned 20:30 bus. I cannot get a home pass, (Keeping rail clear for essential traffic?). Saw *Claudia* at camp cinema.

10 June

I was issued a day pass only, to Wolverhampton, so I went at 10:00 and had a good lunch at a restaurant and then went to two cinemas. Am cheesed-off and lonely.

11 June

I was put on night-flying duty for a week and they flew all night every night, it was hot for sleeping during days.

14 June

Pilotless planes are now reaching Kent and London. I noted them every day thereafter with the first local damage on Gibbon Road.

17 June

My night duties are busy with many radio snags to attend to in the aircraft. I am worried about the doodlebugs on London.

Sunday, 18 June

Although I was expecting an overseas posting at any time, I slipped away without a pass when my night duties ended. I caught buses to Stourbridge, then Birmingham from where I hitched first to Coventry then to London. I was home by 23:00. Hungerford Bridge was hit by a doodlebug. I was due back on B Flight at Halfpenny Green by 08:00 on Monday 19th but friends had agreed to cover for that day. So I saw Grandad, had good meals, (we all ignored the flying bombs), left home at 14:00—Tube to Barnet, bus to St Albans, hitched to Brum, train to Stourbridge and walked from there and under the wire near my hut 23:45 totally shagged out.

Air Raids and RAF Days

I was commanded to appear before the signals officer the next morning, but bowel movement not called for as it was to allocate me a Hillman signals van to drive.

Happier now except for continuous flying bomb raids on London. Mum became a blood donor at Seaman's Hospital, Greenwich.

21 June

Uncle John passed away.

I saw *Jane Eyre* (Orson Welles, Joan Fontaine), good.

Grandad was slightly injured in a local buzz-bomb blast and our remaining ceilings all came down and the furniture was damaged.

I put in for a pass home, but then a C.O.'s Parade was arranged and passes were cancelled. I saw *Madame Curie* instead, Grier Garson, very fine.

[*The London County Council Bomb Damage Maps 1939–1945* record a V1 and V2 very close indeed to St Norbert's Road.]

21 St Norbert Rd
Brockley
SE4
23 June 1944

Dear John,

I am now finding time to write a few lines. As I expect Mum has already told you in letters Uncle John passed away 05:00 Wednesday morning. Mum and I went over to Mitcham Wednesday. Uncle Bill and Aunt Flo were there. [Aunt Flo and Uncle Bill Teague lived at 47 Corporation Road, Croydon].

The funeral is to take place Monday the 26th at 14:30. He is going to be buried in the family grave at Forest Hill. Mum and I will be going also Uncle Bill and Aunt Flo. We received your parcel of washing etc and the bank statements and have put away. Mum sent Alvin a nice birthday card. I thought the extract from the 'Fun page of local government service' funny. Yes we received your health cards and I have put them away. Mum has taken snaps to be done. I was very relieved when we received your letter dated 20 June saying you had arrived back safely.

Mum has become a blood donor and gave the first transfusion Thursday. In these times they need all the transfusions they can get. Do not know if any more news this time. Hoping that you are keeping well with all our best wishes and the best of luck.

Much love from us both. God bless you.

Dad

[*On 24 June, the card index of bomb damage at Lewisham Central Library records slight damage to 21, St Norbert Road and further slight damage on the 27th.*]

21 St Norbert Rd
Brockley
SE4
26 June 1944

My dear son,

In one of my letters I have told you that I had received your laundry last Thursday morning I'm afraid it is not washed yet, I could not do it then because of the blood doings and since then I have spent all my spare time sleeping in between doodlebugs coming over and we have had some. Coming just from the cemetery today eight of the devils came over one dropped at Nunhead somewhere near the library, and the Goldsmiths I think it has got hit in the part they have just started repairing.

It is dreadful the way they come over and you have just got to wait and pray it will not hit your house it is getting us all down. I am afraid I am not a bit brave where they're concerned and the other I am just trying in my own way to help. They tell me I am a good blood donor I have of course got a card.

Poor old Grandad is not well. Poor old dear. We will both keep out of danger as much as we can; I wish they would stop them coming over.

Fondest love, God bless

Mum

Will do your washing in the morning God willing and get it away to you.

21 St Norbert Rd
Brockley
SE4
26 June 1944

Dear John,

Mum and I have just returned from the funeral. We had two alerts before we started from home and the last continued throughout the burial. The all-clear went whilst we were sheltering in the new cemetery. In second raid there were eight that got through. It is certainly very worrying. We received a letter from Auntie Kate about 10 minutes before we started out for the funeral saying that she had been blitzed out of house and home last Thursday morning between 09:00 and 10:00. She is really bearing up wonderfully. I have advised her to try and get away out of it for a change. The funeral was carried out very efficiently and there were some very nice wreaths. I was very pleased you wrote a letter of sympathy.

Yes I know how false the news is about their friendship. Roberts and everybody will be greatly relieved when they know they have been beaten. Your contribution to the wreath is nil as I sent it from us all at Brockley but I appreciate your thoughtful offer.

Yes we should not hesitate to send you a telegram should we need you but please God we shall not. Please do not try to come home as it only makes things more worrying. We both know that you pray for our safety as we both do for your safekeeping.

Hoping that you are keeping well. With all our best wishes and the very best of luck from us both.

God bless you,

Dad

Do not worry.

21, ~~St.~~ Norbert Rd,
Brockley.
S.E.4.
26.6.44.

Dear John,
Mum & I have just returned from the funeral. We had two alerts before we started from home, & the last continued throughout the burial, the all clear went whilst we were sheltering in the new cemetery. In second raid there were eight that got through. It is certainly very worrying. We received a letter from Auntie Kate, about 10. mins. before we started out for the funeral, saying she had been blitzed out of house & home last Thursday morning between 9 & 10. a.m. She is really bearing up wonderfully. I have advised her to try and get away out of it for a change. The funeral was

carried out very efficiently, & there were some very nice wreaths. I was very pleased you wrote a letter of sympathy. Yes I know how false the news is about these fiendish Robots, & everybody will be greatly relieved when they know that they have been beaten. Your contribution to the wreath is nil, as I sent it from us all at Brockley, but I appreciate your thoughtful offer. Yes we should not hesitate to send you a telegram should we need you which please God we shall not. Please do not try to come home, as it only makes things more worrying. We both know that you pray for our safety, as we both do for your safe keeping. Hoping that you are keeping well. With all best wishes & the very best of luck from us both. God bless you. Do not worry. Dad.

21 St Norbert Rd
Brockley
28 June 1944

Dear John,

I am now writing a few lines in answer to your letters of the 25 and 26 June pleased to hear the ENSA show was not too bad. We received a parcel from Ida to you and Mum has posted on to you. The weather here is very dull and the winds are very strong with showers at intervals. It is a good thing to know that you do occasionally get a good dinner and tea.

Hope that you enjoyed Jane Eyre. I have put in an application for a Morrison shelter, as Mum thinks she would feel safer in one, and I think the same. But as you know she has never wanted anything of the sort before. Having a good deal to do with the head of the shelter department, I may be able to get one along fairly quickly. As a rule they take about a fortnight. This robot they are sending over has a very high blasting power and if anything worse than the 1941 blitz.

But you are not to worry as we shall let you know how things are going at every opportunity. It was not necessary to send you a telegram but we will if we should need you at any time.

I have already got a claim form in case we need it but thank God up to the present there is nothing to claim for. Yes as you say those sentences from Flotsam are very true and as you say troubles to all come at once but we have a great deal to be thankful for...

[Next page is missing.]

29 June

I nipped off to Birmingham and saw *For Whom the Bell Tolls* at the Futurist, good food, Y.M.C.A. back 23:59.

2 July

Avignon Road was hit by a flying bomb and Dad worked extra all night seeking people he knew in the rubble.

Syd's civil defence medal certificate.

The air raid wardens at St Catherine's Church, 1945. Syd is in the middle row, seventh from left.

3 July

Night duties this week 19:00 to 07:00, so went to Stourbridge in afternoons for cinema etc. Saw *The Uninvited*. Driving around dispersal points now. Flying bomb raids on London continue.

Sunday, 9 July

Bed after night duty, up at 12:00 and on 14:30 bus to Stourbridge, bus to Birmingham, bus to Coventry, then hitched to Oxford, another to Staines, another to Kensington, underground and tram home by 23:45. More flying bombs. Damage is severe. Saw Grandad. A letter came from Uncle Bill, they are bombed out.

10 July

Back by midnight, covered by friends, no pass. Letter from Jimmy Booker, with wedding photograph, he is posted overseas.

11 July

Nasty prang, poor sods. Camp cinema, saw Bette Davis *Now Voyager*, well-acted. Mother and Father at last have a minimal air raid shelter a Morrison, no good for anything very close though. London is still being bombed all the time.

14–21 July

Chaps are being posted and we are shorthanded on Flight. I was put on A Flight and serviced radios all day 07:00 to 19:00, for a week.

22 July

I was rewarded with a day pass, but only to Birmingham. Stayed Y.M.C.A. Good food, Sutton Coldfield Park, girls and fun fair, back on 21:00 bus to Stourbridge, the last one. On the Friday there had been an unsuccessful attempt to assassinate Hitler. We talked about it for hours and decided it would not affect us.

Cranwell Again

26 July

I was posted immediately to Cranwell once more for a 'B.A.' course (British Aviation) to start 07:00 the next morning. A nice W.A.A.F. in H.Q. made my rail pass out via London and I was home to a lovely meal without warning and off early evening to Lincoln. I got there so late that I had to pay for a taxi to Cranwell 30/-. The course was interesting and I was able to hear music in the evening (*Swan Lake* and

Beethoven). I now know nobody here. The Buzz-Bomb Blitz on London continues.

I came top in the B.A. theory examination for my course. ENSA show in evening.

Sunday, 30 July

I visited Lincoln alone, Cathedral (again), the Bishops Palace and the jail (1872), a reminder of the brutality of those recent days. Cinema saw *This Man Reuter*. Met a Mona acquaintance and got pissed.

1 August

Arica Road, Cranfield Road, Marks and Spencer Lewisham hit. Exam on B.A. equipment.

2 August

Terrific raid, 81 reached and exploded in South London.

Sunday, 6 August

Lincoln alone, fed at Y.M.C.A. saw film of childhood favourite Fennimore Cooper *Last of Mohicans*. I had to stay for Boards, which I passed well. Raids on London continued. Posted back to Halfpenny Green, took rail warrant back to Orderly Room and got it marked 'via London'. Home for one hour, house even more blast damaged, parents 'stiff upper-lips'. Halfpenny Green by 23:59—made it.

10 August

Flight servicing with van this week, warm. Letter from Jimmy in Africa. To Stourbridge and Brum in evening. *Fanny by Gaslight*, Phyllis Calvert, not bad, with a W.A.A.F.. It got too late to get back, Y.M.C.A. was full, had to go to Dale End Hostel. War news is good.

Sunday, 13 August

In evening to Odeon David Niven *The Way Ahead*, adjustment of civilians to service life, true to life.

15 August

Invasion of Southern France, which really should shorten war, blitz on London continues.

16 August

I was put on a battle course firing a rifle and Sten gun with and without a respirator, throwing grenades. The following day I fired a Bren gun.

19–25 August

I was sent on embarkation leave. The early part of the week was filled with air raid alerts day and night, so I tried out the table shelter. I fixed boards from a bombed house in Arica Road over our kitchen window so that they could put a light on in the night (replacing the boards I had put up before, which are now shattered).

I wrote to Grandad who is in Grimsby staying with McKay relatives. I sorted lots of my things out for disposal and sold one of the violins that Uncle John had left me (blast damaged at Brockley) in Gerard Street for £5 (it was a Chipot Viullaume, 1891). I also sold some of my parent's old gramophone records in Charing Cross Road for 5/-.

I took Mother to the Lewisham Gaumont to see *This Happy Breed* in Technicolor. There were several raid-free days and nights.

27 August–3 September

When I got back to Halfpenny Green they told me that I should have been given 14 days embarkation leave not seven and sent me home again. I was home by 02:19 on 28 August.

In that week, I sold two old fountain pens for 5/-, saw *For Whom the Bell Tolls* for the second time at the Rivoli, went to Lewisham to buy Dad a coach ticket to Hastings as Mother and I decided he must have a couple of days break if she stayed in the house. He is completely shagged.

Lewisham shopping centre is devastated by doodlebug explosions, what is left is boarded up but still operating. Dad said I had wasted my money. He would not go and told me off for swearing at him.

Then a policeman called with an R.A.F. telegram. I was to report back on 4 September for an earlier draft overseas to a Forward Staging Post, number 18 of Transport Command, which made Mother cry, so I went straight away.

Lyneham, Wiltshire

4 September

I was issued with Air Force blue battle dress, a Sten gun, two blankets, etc. and the next day I was taken to Wolverhampton and then given a train pass to Swindon, I stood all the way on a crowded train and at Swindon I was collected by R.A.F. bus and taken to the airfield from which I visited Cricklade several evenings for drinks and one Sunday to go to church.

I later noted: By 4 September 1944, Antwerp was liberated by the British 8th Army. The Germans were taken completely by surprise at the speed of the advance and one of their generals wrote of it as an 'impossible' four-day 250-mile dash by British armoured forces. Amiens, Arras, Tournai, Brussels and Louvain were taken on the way. We could not use the port of Antwerp, however, for the Germans remained in considerable strength on each side of the estuary.

Brussels, Belgium

[Note added by John years later from a document at the National Archives[1]:]

---

1 NA/AIR 38/238 & 239 and AIR 38/111

Group Captain John Bradbury wrote: 18 Terminal Staging Post arrived in Brussels, taking up its quarters on the old Brussels-Everre airport on 3 September, the day of the liberation of the city. The Germans, having retained possession of all the Channel ports and the road communications by reason of their length, being quite incapable of dealing with the supply situation. Air transport at this juncture really came into its own. From September until early October, the Brussels-Everre airport (B.56) handled between 400 and 500, and often more, Dakota transport aircraft a day, while more than 1,000 tons of petrol and ammunition were loaded and unloaded and sent forward in an endeavour to keep the armies on the move... his tremendous traffic strained the resources of 18 staging post to the utmost, since the unit was only designed to handle 200 tons of freight a day. The work would in fact have been impossible without the willing cooperation of the R.A.S.C. who not only performed their function of unloading and disposing of the army freight, but also helped with the loading of casualties into the empty aircraft for transport to the U.K.

17 September

I was flown by Dakota direct to Everre Airfield, Brussels, and the same evening became part of extraordinary celebrations in the City centre. I had four gins at 40 francs and 11 small beers; the latter purchased for me by grateful Belgians of all ages. I passed from drunk back to very sober. At the airfield we seized Luftwaffe food stores, all tinned: bacon, already cooked in rashers wound round each other with paper, very fat, had lots every day, but also loads of grapes at 48 francs for four litres. I had to sleep in an aircraft hangar, on the ground, on my rubber groundsheet with my two blankets.

We also had to guard R.A.F. equipment and stores all night, but I believe one of us was awake at any one moment and we were all armed with loaded Sten guns.

Douglas C47 Dakota No. ZA947 of the R.A.F. Battle of Britain Memorial Flight on final approach at R.A.F. Coningsby, Lincolnshire

18 September

The next day all English currency silver had to be handed in, in exchange for Belgian francs. I was given 150 for 17/-. The next evening, I went into the city and met Lucille, who could not speak a word of English. I exercised my school French and learned three words in Flemish. She was 18, a charming girl, we walked talked, kissed etc. and I gave her chocolate for her family.

19 September

I was duty mechanic and got soaked working on an aircraft right across the airfield (our vehicles had not arrived).

I was able to go into Brussels again, this time sightseeing, with a cinema in the evening (*The Rains Came*), excellent French dialogue. It was then late and I had to repel persistent prostitutes who wanted payment in English cigarettes.

20 September

I barged straight into the Parc Theatre and saw Ivor Novello in *Love From A Stranger*. There I met a middle-aged man, a teacher, who offered to improve my French for cigarettes. I told him my unit was mobile and I would be in Holland soon (our paratroops had invaded Holland by air) and that he would do better with someone stationed in Brussels.

There was no night flying, so I had every evening off in town, seeing films such as *Au Service D'Autre*, *The Lamp Still Burns*, *Wuthering Heights*, (with Flemish dialogue and Flemish captions!). I found a serviceman's club and saw an ENSA show *Going My Way*. My first overseas pay parade yielded 525 Belgian francs. I started getting mail from home, via our 46 Group aircraft, no doubt, but sorted elsewhere.

I learned that Mother had had a bad fall and hurt her hand needing seven stitches.

Envelope dated 27 September 1944.

21 St Norbert Rd
Brockley
30 September 1944

My dear son,

I am trying to write a few lines to you. I expect you have got Dad's letter telling you that I have injured my right hand rather badly have got seven stitches in it and it is hurting like hell. I have put in a claim at the Town Hall don't know if I shall get anything but I have to pay the hospital a small sum shall claim for panel. Hope you can understand this. I'm enclosing a letter from Ida. Will send Observer tomorrow. Dad is being very kind and helpful. I cannot do a thing for myself. The neighbours almost all kind except the 'snake one'. Mrs Gibling has cleaned right through and comes in every morning to help me. Dad is on early turn, she also comes to hospital with me.

God bless you
Fondest love Mum
Fancy going through the air raids and then getting this.

Sunday, 1 October

I went to a local pub with Bert Perry and met Simone. Very sweet. I exercised my French; his girl was appropriately older. The next night I was duty mechanic on alone, so I explored the German ammunition dumps and stole a revolver as a souvenir, but decided against ammunition, not wishing to break a box open. The next afternoon, I was off-duty and went to Brussels with Bob (a Canadian corporal), to cinema to see Diana Durbin *It's a Date*. Then had a good time eats, drinks, girls.

2 October

I introduced Bob to the Pare Theatre, but was not allowed to barge in again, but very politely asked to pay. Bob paid; his Canadian rates of pay are much better! We saw Shaw's *Arms and the Man*. The next night I was duty mechanic and I found it advisable to point my loaded Sten gun at a scruffy Belgian who appeared near the kite I was servicing.

He only wanted he said in slow clear French to give me a bottle of cognac. Yes he would take some English cigarettes. He did and I made him bugger off smartish away from the aircraft. I became hooked on cognac and always called for it in bars thereafter. Indeed on our Saturday night out I introduced Bob to it and we both got roaring drunk and spent all our money.

Eindhoven, Holland

21 St Norbert Rd
Brockley
6 October 1944

My dear son,

In answer to your letter of the 1st I would like to tell you first that I was discharged from hospital this morning. My hand is still very sore but apart from the bandage on thumb and palm of hand I can now use my fingers. Doctor says I ought to be able to use my hand properly in a fortnight if I practice.

I went to Jones this afternoon with your pen and the young lady did not hold out a lot of hope about getting it repaired but will let me know in three weeks' time she asked if you would like a new one if the other would not be done. I should think that those letters of Ida's must have been written some time ago else why should they be censored when our local papers are full with pictures of the bomb damage? I have sent Ida two recent Kentish Mercurys I shall now be anxious to get a letter from her to see if they have been destroyed.

I should like to see the Wuthering Heights I have not been anywhere for the last three weeks Dad was so worried about my silly old hand. We thought of going to Lewisham Hippodrome next week to see Eddie Gray with the Crazy Gang it should be very funny. Your fruit and walnut sounds very tempting. It seems funny to us here that the girls over there are so well dressed and we are all getting so shabby. Eddie Lahaise, Kitty's husband is moving your way and he's going to look out for you.

I shall have to wait a good while for repairs if only they would see to roof and brickwork we had another fall of bricks I think it was dangerous but others don't so it is not much use worrying. I expect you will get those papers you spoke of shortly. Dad is getting one of the part timers who work in London to get them for him. I have got your 'Library Assistant' will send it in The Observer. It has turned cold and we are glad of a fire it has not rained today that's something to be thankful.

God bless you my dear take care of yourself try and keep clear of colds. Dad has one in his head not bad but he feels sorry for himself.

Fondest love, Mum and Dad xxxxxx

Air Raids and RAF Days

[John added these further notes from the National Archives documents written by Group Captain Bradbury:]

On 8 October the unit moved to Eindhoven. The battle situation was very fluid at this time and it was noted that the unit stood to on the 9th for one and a half hours ready to repel a possible German attack.

Sunday, 8 October

The next morning, our vehicles caught up with us, I took over a three-ton signals workshop (a Bedford) and in the early evening, everything being ready we drove to Eindhoven, it was very, very wet and pitch dark. I drove often on narrow lanes between white tapes, with roadside graves, German and allied with helmet and identity disc hung on a wooden cross (temporary, to be reburied later).

The noise of battle was clearly audible (35 kilometres away, however). We were issued with our first rum ration and slept on the bombed airfield at Eindhoven, Holland. The next night we set up tents in the wood beside the airfield. General duties airmen laid a steel strip runway, filling craters as they went.

The following day our 46 Group Dakotas landed on it, these were refuelled and serviced as necessary on the way to England with released allied prisoners of war. (My New Zealand second cousin Winston Condor was one and he stayed in my house, in my bed, shortly afterwards). There were also badly wounded personnel from the front and WRNC nurses tended them.

On the outward journey the Dakotas carried medical supplies etc. Flights of Mosquito (wooden) aircraft, two-engined fighters carried out daylight raids on Berlin to speed the end of the war. These landed and refuelled. They had napalm tanks to drop on Berlin fitted underneath their wings. Some had to land on way back. Oh Gawd!

The rum ration continued, Dutch weather, pelting rain continued, our tents leaked and all our possessions got wet. We started cooking extras, in a clearing in the wood, potatoes and German-tinned bacon boiled in German aluminium halves of mine cases over a wood fire kindled with petrol and I boiled my underwear, shirts and woollen socks, all together. We dried them strung in vans. Guarding everything was continuous for all.

Mosquito

12 October

Bob, Windle (Windy) and I walked into Eindhoven, had one beer, all they could spare for they had had a very tough time, then to a worker's home for coffee. It was ersatz, made from acorns. Ugh! His kindness was rewarded with quite a few cigarettes and several bars of nutritious R.A.F.-issue chocolate. The next day I had an Anson to service and then visited Eindhoven alone (with Sten gun), to different worker's house for coffee.

Sunday, 15 October

We had an airfield church service, C. of E. We dispensed with the parade. I gave silent thanks for our successes. I am reading Housman, *The Shropshire Lad*, bought in Swindon, now very soggy. Letters, *Observers* and several *New Statesman* arrived from home. In addition to the Dakotas, Ansons, etc., I now also service the TR9s in the Flying Control Van.

18 October

I was given permission to fill my van with chaps and drive to Eindhoven Swimming Baths. There with hundreds of soldiers, we washed ourselves in what was a swimming bath in HOT water. The wet weather continued and in the evenings, we walked into Eindhoven to an ENSA cinema that had been set up to see *Gentleman Jim*. One of my additional servicing jobs was to install a V.H.F. set in a Dakota that unaccountably did not have one!

Diest, Belgium

21 St Norbert Rd
Brockley
20 October 1944

My dear son,

We are OK. Today I have good news for you; I was discharged from hospital. The electric treatment shortwave has reduced the nasty swelling. I've been going every day for the last 3 ½ weeks and I have now got the bandage off apart from nasty scars and feeling stiff and sore it's OK.

I hope you won't mind I have cut the fingers out of one of your old grey-blue gloves. I've got to keep my hand covered for the time being indoors as well as out.

About the compensation, there is nothing doing at the Town Hall. They sent me a letter saying that they much regretted my accident, but the pavement was in ordinary wear and tear — the blighters.

I got Dad to send a letter on to the Co-op Insurance who with the doctor are acting in my interest. I had a letter from them telling me that I would have extreme difficulty in sustaining a claim for damages and advising me to let the matter drop and they would arrange for sickness benefit for me to be authorised. As Dad has seen to all this business for me, he's writing tonight to accept benefit for me, so that's that will save all the letters and show you one day.

I am sending you two forms. Hope they are what you wanted. Let. me know then I can send on more. Hope you have now got your scarf. I expect we shall hear from you soon but this letter will be posted early.

Just now there was an awful loud bang no warning. It shook the place. I had to laugh. I've never seen your Billy move so quick before. His fur all stood up along his back and he glared at me as if it were my fault.

Well, Dad will be in for his supper in a few moments. He does not seem to get rid of his cold. I think he has been worrying about me. By the way I have just sent Ida's insurance policy off to her registered. Dad got it transferred to Canada after a lot of silly red tape.

Please take care of yourself, dear. Although the leaves are falling my rose tree is still in bud and there are one or two marigolds in flower and others.

God bless you my dear and may he keep his protecting arms around you.

Fondest love from Mum and Dad don't worry about me. Am feeling nearly fit now. xxxx

24 October

We moved back to Diest in Belgium. A little town with a ruined castle on a mound, a garlic-and-glow-worm-filled wood between us and the town. (First time I have seen glow-worms glowing, uncanny). A few beers in the town; set up tents on an estate. In afternoon off next day explored Diest with Bob, Windy, and Phil (Jones). Had cream cakes and coffee. Bought souvenirs. At this time the V1 flying bombs often went over us (from mobile launchers) on their way to further devastate London and Kent.

26 October

Into Diest in evening to spend all my remaining Belgian money on cakes, ice-cream and Dodgem cars at a fair set up in a town square. I provided this plus beer for my canny Welsh colleague Phil Jones, who always managed to have no money, or all Dutch when he needed Belgian, or all English when he needed Dutch. He never repaid.

It was in Diest that I found a shop with Optimiste perfume and I bought a bottle for Mother. (The Germans had kept the Brussels area as a leave centre with goods still in the shops, not like poor Holland).

On the Saturday night I met up with a charming girl in Diest, not cumbered with friends. I had had a lot of cognac and some real port that had been hoarded. *Un peu de mushing*!

We were so wet and had been for so long that we arranged among ourselves to cover duties for each other.

[John later added a note from the National Archive document]:

28 October the Air Officer commanding wrote: 'Whilst it is true that at peak periods 18 staging Post at B. 56 established to handle 200 tons per day, actually handled on one or two days over 1,000 in good weather, 800 in poor, it had been proved that during the wet winter months no airfield could be used extensively unless it had hard runways...few airfields had those intact. Even the airfield at Brussels (Everre) which has been looked upon as the one to be used for intensive air transport operations, had gone unserviceable and could not be re-opened until the concrete strip had been extended accordingly, I propose to withdraw 18 Staging Post to Britain as soon as accommodation can be found to receive it.'

30 October

Early evening, Bob Fielder, the Canadian corporal and I decamped to Brussels in my signals tender. What a risk!

What an adventure! We got pissed on cognac and could not remember where the van was, so we booked into Hotel Royal, 119 Boulevard Maurice Lemonnier, 50 francs each for the night. We had more booze and then to cinema *The Amazing Mr. Williams*. At Diest we were waved in to avoid problems at 08:30 next morning.

Parcels from home at this time included candles 1 lb at a time, torch batteries and food.

Life continued under canvas at Diest with a rum ration for a time.

Sunday, 5 November

I hitched a lift into Louvain in an Army lorry. I found the centre shelled and bombed flat including the university library that had been destroyed by the Germans in the last war also. I went to a cinema to get dry and warm and saw *You Can't Take It With You*, with French and Flemish captions. It took quite a while to get lifts back to Diest, driving first, into France to Lille.

6 November

I responded to letters from Guy and Jimmy, took a written trade board for promotion and played solo, winning 140 Belgian francs.

7 November

An air letter from Ida (of 27 October) informed me that Alvin was being unfaithful to her. She is obviously very shaken. On my next visit to Diest I bought Mother miniature souvenir sabots and an embroidered handkerchief.

8 November

An Army mobile bath unit visited us by arrangement. Lovely hot water. Then there was pay parade at which I got 525 Belgian francs. Then I drove off in Ray's lorry to Brussels, without a pass. To the top of the Congress Column, into the cathedral, then to a news cinema followed by Churchill Theatre *Hunchback of Notre Dame*, Laughton, then to an excellent café bar, much cognac and on to the usual hotel, too pissed to drive back to Diest.

Pep talk next day from C.O. about discipline and our scruffy appearance. We weren't backward in telling him that we were not sleeping in a chateau as he was, but on tomato boxes on the wet earth. He soon shut up, implying that we were marvellous chaps. Snow.

9 November

I wired some lights to the cookhouse tent from a mobile generator. I am reading *Politics Made Plain* T.L. Horabin, as well as *Observer* and *New Statesman* posted from home. Knowing that we were about to move up again, I bought Christmas presents for Mother and Ida 4711 face powder (German), stockings and a silver necklet (125 and 150 Belgian francs, financed by selling my cigarette ration).

21 St Norbert Rd
Brockley
11 November 1944

My dear son,

Thank you for your kind and tactful letter today. Poor Ida she is having her peck of trouble. I have sent her an airmail and posted it as soon as I read your letter. Of course, we are both very upset. Dad has taken it very much to heart. He's very fond of her although she would never believe it.

I told her to come home there would always be a loving welcome here from both of us. You do me an injustice when you think I should scold her. I knew before she went to Canada that he was telling her lies when he said he had been in Canada House. In fact I was told he was playing a funny game.

No names but it was no use telling Dad, so I kept quiet. Ida told me herself that the woman where they stayed told her Mac was no good and of course Ida rowed with her over it.

Did you know that they had brought a bill in here where girls can get a divorce in this country even if their husbands are in another country? Dad seems to think there is a chance that they might come together again.

What I want to know is if she has gone out to work as I have had a parcel from her posted 20 September got it 9 November can she be short of money?

Do you want me to go to Barclays again? Perhaps I might be lucky this time? Let me know I don't mind what I do if I can help her. Don't worry about the rockets we are OK. They have not been very near us. Do you remember that boy

Shardeloes who went to St Donats? It was near where he lived.

Dad is writing to you but I thought might you might like to hear what we both had to say about Ida separately.

Billy is hugging the fire. I am going to try another shop for your Christmas Carol, also Bleak House. I bet you just hated writing that letter. I will try not to worry.

By the way, I told Ida that I would not say anything and would leave it for her to do what she thought best when she came home. They ought to send the dirty blighter to fight the Japs. Glad she had the guts to show him up to his C.O.

I hope his name stinks. He should be an officer perhaps it's gone to his head.

Well now, don't you worry.

God bless you and keep you safe
Fondest love
Mum

21 St Norbert Rd
Brockley
12 November 1944

Dear John,

I received your letter dated 7 November yesterday afternoon, saying you had now received The Observer of 22 October, New Statesman and Spectator. We are both very worried about Ida and do not think it at all unnatural that she should write to you asking you to break the news. Mum sent off an airmail letter as soon as we had read your letter to her saying that she would always find a home with us. Until we hear from Ida, I don't see what steps we can take in the matter and you think she's apparently in good hands.

We had been thinking of writing to his parents to see what they intend to do about things but shall wait till we hear either from you or Ida so that we are able to work on something definite.

Surely there is a law guarding these young and inexperienced wives from having their lives blasted.

Anyway, we shall not do anything in the matter until we hear again from you saying what you think is the best course to take. Unfortunately, we are such a distance away that it takes such a time before we hear from one another. We certainly should not suggest a reconciliation.

Mum put in her letter to Ida that there would be a loving welcome from both of us. Do not upset yourself too much about events, as things might turn out better than we expected. Mum has sent a letter off to you also The Observer. Do not know that I can say any more this time.

Hoping that we shall get better news of Ida. I do not know if you mean you are trying to send Ida money for her fare. If so don't you think it should come from the other *side by the authorities on compassionate grounds?*

Hoping that you are keeping well. With all our best wishes and the very best of luck.

Much love from us both.

God bless and keep you,

Dad

16 November

We packed up and moved to Nivelles. Arriving late afternoon, we took over a blasted building, the Ecole Normale or teachers' training college. We had a nun's cubicle each. Quite like home, as no glass left in windows. Very cold weather, nothing to do as we are waiting to go forward. Cafes to keep warm most of day and late into the night, I found one that had hidden a barrel of real port in its cellar all through occupation, now selling at 15 francs a glass straight from the barrel. I took a new arrival, Joe Bagley, (an older chap rather stout, who shambles rather than walks, a history teacher lately called up) to this cafe the day he arrived and we became firm friends.

We drank a great deal; I believe that he was a nonconformist teetotaller like myself, only he was breaking out at about the age of 39. The next morning, he chatted up the signals officer to convey us both to Waterloo in his Jeep (the S.O. on his way to visit his mistress in Brussels). The site of the battle came alive with Joe talking about the location of each army in the battle, viewed from the top of the monument.

A local, seeing us up there, came out and sold us pre-war postcards. We were allowed into the closed-up panorama (no lights) and later walked to several H.Q.s of the armies. An excellent day. Not so funny getting back, quite near but hard to find (no signs of course, except military unit signs and not ours).

Candles from home proved to be very useful, as there was no electricity that worked. (Other chaps less organised than I was did not steal them but sometimes took one from my kit bag when I was out, leaving a token payment).

21 St Norbert Rd
Brockley

11 November 1944

My dear son,

Sorry I have not written before but I was not feeling too good. I have had a good many headaches lately. I think all this noise is bad at times for all of us but worse for you boys. We are worrying at hearing on the wireless that you are getting those damn rockets and doodlebugs. We pray God will keep you safe.

I am going to Jones in the morning to see if your book is in so expect will not post this until I see if I have got it. Shall I send you some more candles?

No, I think the parcel was intended for me with the idea that I could make you a cake and pudding to send to you. As you know we are not allowed to send food parcels, so as soon as I can get some suet I am going to make a pudding to save for when you can get home on leave. It had two packets of Sun-Maid raisins, jellies, cheese, two bars of chocolate, hairpins and some steel wool for cleaning.

As Dad has already told you it is true about that picture, there are a lot of people out of work already, so it is certainly up to you boys to stand together over these things. The other day there was a case in a paper about a firm who had taken a married ex-serviceman back and wanted to pay him pre-war money 35/-. They were ordered to pay £4. I will bet they will do all they can to get rid of him.

Pleased to know you understand about the 30/-. No I shall not keep an account what I spend for you, you have been very generous to me dear, let me do what I can to repay a little.

I got my boots and shoes mended and got myself a new woollen dress with that insurance money and things I wanted.

So you enjoyed your air trip, what an experience. Yes we are now waiting rather anxiously to hear from Ida.

I am sorry to tell you that when my hand was getting a bit better and Dad was coming into dinner I upset some fat on Billyboy and burnt him a bit. It did upset me as you know I would not hurt him for anything the fur has just come off and I think it will soon heal He was a brave boy but he will get in the way. It is on his side and if I put anything he licks it off.

When I wrote last to Auntie Flo I gave her your address so you might hear from her.

I have got Dad to buy some milk and oil and I'm going to see he takes it; he's jibbing a bit I'm hoping it will stop him getting a bad cold like he had last winter when it sets in cold.

The weather is still very wet and very mild I have just heard that USO show on the wireless coming from Paris with Fred Astaire and a hot club affair, what a noise are you able to listen in?

Saturday, 25th

Well I could not get A Christmas Carol, but they had Bleak House so I got that for you hope you will like it. I have sent it off by registered post so you should get it soon but was only able to get one of your papers so I have enclosed in parcel wrapped round a book.

I went down this morning for the book but first went to Woolworths and Kennedys opposite the Town Hall I had just got home by tram again when a damn rocket came down on Woolworths it's pretty bad Dad says. I was very lucky it shook me up a bit when I realised things.

Fondest love to you.
God bless you,
Mum and Dad xxx

Bomb damage at Woolworth's New Cross. The V2 killed 168 people (courtesy of Lewisham Heritage, Lewisham Council).

24 November

I was officially allowed to drive a truckload of chaps to Brussels. I saw Conrad Veidt *The Man They Could Not Hang*. Many cognacs; drove them back without incident. The next day most of us had hot baths at the Civil Hospital, arranged by our own M.O. Later Joe and I over many beers met a local schoolmaster with a good command of English and he was patient with my French. The next evening Joe and I went with Stan Walker (a very quiet corporal, who hardly speaks), to meet his friends in a café bar. One is a baker, the other a tobacconist, he wants our cigarettes of course, excellent boozy evening, also with delicious Belgian pastries. Lots of slow French conversation.

The next evening several local wizard females sought our company and we had a very enjoyable time.

29 November

I drove to Brussels without authority in the evening taking Bob Fielder and Stan Walker and spent loads of money getting pissed.

1 December

We packed up everything early in the wagons and drove them to a Brussels airfield, Maelsbruk, where we left them under guard and flew off in a flight of '46' Group Dakotas direct to Perranporth in Cornwall, a flight of three and a quarter hours just above the clouds.

The German Ardennes offensive looks about to smash through into most of Belgium and the invasion of Holland at Arnhem has failed.

Perranporth, Cornwall

The landing of our kite was clearly a bit hairy with two attempts before making it. The cliff edge hurtled up to us and we roared up and round again until on the third approach he risked dropping on to the ground with a God Almighty thump. As we were sitting on the floor sideways along the fuselage, some got nasty bumps on pretty raw aluminium struts. I enjoyed it, not believing that I would die then.

Some chaps were actually sick. Nissan huts were ready for us, with stoves glowing, floor polished and beds in neat rows, then to the cookhouse for a very good meal. To St Agnes over the cliff path to the cinema in the evening in a gale. I wrote home from England to their immense surprise.

I immediately fell in love with Cornwall, the wild gales and enormous surfy seas, the caves and the food!

21 St Norbert Rd
Brockley

1 December 1944

Dear John,

It is just a year ago today since Ida said goodbye to me over the phone what a lot has happened since then.

I hope you will have got my registered parcel by now and like contents.

I am sending a parcel off to you on Monday it will be 'ropes for ball' otherwise a cake. I am sending it to you in the tin it was baked in don't you worry about throwing it away when you're done with the cake. I bought it for that purpose hope your 'mice' won't nibble it, so look out for it. I don't suppose I should be able to register it.

We have had a very cheerful letter from Ida she has started work and is going to live with another girl. I'm rather pleased to think she is going to cut herself adrift from the other lot. She speaks about going to parties only hope and pray in the reaction she will keep her head and not do anything foolish. I expect she will write and tell you more. I'm going to declare your parcel books as you already know we have to sign the form stuck on the parcel.

Well your Billy is going on OK. Hope you are keeping well.

God bless you, dear.

Fondest love,

Mum xxx

4 December

I sent Grandad a belated 85th birthday card. The NAAFI supplied us each with four oranges for 9d. St Agnes saw me each evening and there was a dear old lady who entertained three or four of us to music in her tiny cottage (one room and kitchen downstairs). She played the viola and piano very well indeed and this was followed by eggs and chips, or eggs bacon and chips, or Cornish pasties, all washed down copiously with tea.

She loved to talk politics and about what we would do after the war. I was very well informed from my diet of *Observer* and *New Statesman* opinions, so we got on like a house on fire. Her cottage was never locked, night or day. She did not charge us for the food, and we thought of her as an angel in disguise.

There was an excellent Methodist canteen in Perranporth and a cinema there as well as in St Agnes. Apart from pay parade I had to attend signals workshop in a perfunctory sort of way and repaired private radio sets for officers, fitting R.A.F. valves as required.

One day Jones said he would come to Redruth with me. Outside I discovered that he had money only for the outward bus, so we explored the town and walked back (Welsh peasant!).

I received a Christmas present from Mother that had been to Europe and back: *Bleak House* and a diary, together with a homemade cake and some candles! So I used the brown paper to send her some dirty European laundry.

21 St Norbert Rd
Brockley

4 December 1944

My dear son,

We are delighted you are in Blighty again but what a pity I did not get it first post I have just sent a cake off to Holland. What can you do about it?? Have you got your Christmas present I sent earlier Bleak House? I registered it. I will take your washing to the laundry as soon as it arrives. We had a nasty bomb affair in the New Cross Road on Woolworths direct hit on the 25 November. There are over 200 dead 270 injured it happened on a busy Saturday morning there a lot of Brockley people killed and a lot of still missing there is a mass funeral this afternoon.

Shall I get your bedroom ready for you what do you think?

I will write to Cheshunt I only had a letter in answer to one of mine this morning saying they are looking forward to seeing you again. It will make a nice outing for us all and we should get a very warm welcome. I am sending Ida's last letter on to you. We are longing to see you. I have made four Christmas puddings and some mustard pickle.

Fondest love.

God bless and keep you,

Mum and Dad xx

Air Raids and RAF Days

> 21 St Norbert Rd
> Brockley
> SE4
>
> Dec: 4^d 44
>
> My dear Son,
>
> We are delighted you are in Blighty again, but what a pity I did not get it first. I have just sent a cake off to Holland, what can you do about it???
>
> Have you got your Xmas present I sent called "Bleak House". I registered it. I will take your washing as soon as it arrives.
>
> We had a nasty bomb affair in New X Rd on Woodpecker, direct hit on 25 Nov, there are over 200 dead
>
> 270 injured, it happened on a busy Saturday morning, there are a lot of Brockley people killed, and a lot still missing, there is a mass funeral this afternoon. Shall I get your bedroom ready for you, what do you think?
>
> I will write to Herbert, I only had a letter in answer to one of mine this morning, saying they are looking forward to seeing you again.
>
> I will make a nice outing for us all and we shall get a very warm welcome.
>
> I am sending Isaac's last letter on to you. We are longing to see you
>
> I have made 4 Xmas puddings and some mustard pickle
>
> fondest love
> God Bless and keep you
> Mum & Dad
> XX XXX XX

The letter above written by Maude.

278

21 St Norbert Rd
Brockley

1 December 1944

Dear John,

We were both very much bucked when we received your letter of 3 December saying you were back in England and you can feel sure how we are both looking forward to seeing you. Mum wrote to you directly she received your letter. It was good to hear that for a change things were well organised and that the boys were pleased with the arrangements. I was sorry to hear about the accident with the cognac but I am pleased to hear your other presents are safe. I should think the country where you are is very rugged and picturesque.

At last I have been able to get a copy of A Christmas Carol by Charles Dickens for you it is a very nice copy with eight illustrations in colour and large print which makes it easy reading. One of the wardens was able to get it for me. It is second hand but in very good condition. Now you must let me know whether I should send it on to you or keep it till you get home.

Hoping that you are still keeping well with all our best wishes and the very best of luck much love from us both.

God bless and keep you,

Dad

S. J. Teague

The letter and envelope written by Syd.

21 St Norbert Rd
Brockley
7 December 1944

My dear son,

Received a second letter from you written on the 5th, also parcel with washing don't worry I will see to it. We are both longing to see your dear face again.

We had a big post today six letters in one day. One from you, two from Ida, one a birthday card to Dad one from Connie enclosing Christmas card, two from Grimsby one from Grandad, he was 85 on the 5th and one from cousin Jesse Mckay where he is staying.

Ida says that she has sent off four parcels to me since September. Up to the present I have only received one expect the other three will turn up. Dad is seeing about the port and sherry for you will do his best there should be three parcels at BLA for you, one lot candles one book and one cake sent 4 December. Will not send Ida's letter on you can see it when you come home. I shall answer it also Connie's. The weather here is damp and cooler although I expect you'll think it warm compared with what you have had.

Our love to you.

God bless and protect you,

Mum

21 St Norbert Rd
Brockley
8 December 1944

Dear John,

We received your letter dated 5 December which Mum answered yesterday, Thursday, also parcel of laundry. Yes I expect the boys are excited after being away since June. The scenery must be very lovely I see by my tourist guide there are many objects of interest in the locality including Perran Round, a curious amphitheatre of considerable size and great antiquity.

I do not think I should trouble to phone unless it was something important you want us to know as we seem to get post fairly regular. Mum will get washing done so that it will be ready for you when on leave.

I am trying to get a bottle of sherry and port. Mum has gone to have her hair done this afternoon. I expect I shall be sending **The Statesman** and **Spectators** on to you this evening.

Hoping that you are still keeping well and are able to see the places of interest while you are there.

With all our best wishes and the very best of luck.

Much love from us both. God bless and keep you.

Dad

19 December

I was given leave from today and welcomed to Brockley by a rocket bomb at 22:00 this evening.

20 December

I went to Lewisham to buy shoes and then to New Zealand House for documentation that my ex-prisoner N.Z. cousin needed. I acquired by persistence. There were more V2s throughout my leave, all in S.E. London.

27 December

To Cheshunt with Mum and Dad to the Gurnetts' place, (old family friends) nice chicken lunch, enjoyable, they made much of me and my exploits. Before leaving to return to Perranporth, I acquired a bottle of rum for Dad as a Christmas present, I chatted up Mr Friend at the off-licence and paid over the odds.

That leave I read *A Christmas Carol* and *Bleak House* by Dickens and *Experiences of an Irish R.M.*, Somerville and Ross.

Sayings copied into the front of my 1944 diary:

If you have only two pence, buy with one a loaf, with the other flowers, for the loaf will keep you alive, the flowers will give you something to live for.~ *Chinese proverb.*

To defend the weak; to resist the oppressor; to add to courage humility; to give to man the service and to God the glory; is the student's duty now; as it was once the duty of the knight.

~Bulwer Lytton, 1852, opening Manchester Public Library.

Books read during 1944 included Wilkie Collins, *The Moonstone* Housman, *The Shropshire Lad*: Sir William Beveridge, *Full Employment in a Free Society.*

1945

During the setback of the Ardennes Offensive, we at R.A.F. Perranporth, had parades twice a day, whilst waiting our return to Europe. In between, I had daily inspections to carry out on aircraft radio installations, Dakotas and Ansons. The weather was cold with gales and snow alternating and I was glad not to be in Eindhoven. I did lots of walking and reading. One outing was Stan Walker's 21st birthday booze-up in a Perranporth hotel. I had far too many gin and tonics but walked back OK.

11 January

Bought Mother 19 eggs at 3/1d a dozen. The farmer supplied a stout cardboard box and lots of newspaper, packed up and posted. Received some mail from last September, decided to give the cake to seagulls.

I was granted leave from 20:25, seat on train but could not sleep, home 07:00 next day to bacon and two eggs breakfast, then to bed for three hours. When I could sleep the next night there was a loud local explosion followed by an alert so we got up and played pontoon and I won 9/1d after several hours.

At 10:00 the next morning, Dad and I took the train to London Bridge and we did one of his 'famous city walks'. I was shagged out. The next day they took me to the Regal Old Kent Road to see Bette Davis in *Old Acquaintance* (not too good).

18 January

I got them to treat me to *Puss in Boots* at the Empire (I'm a great baby, living in the past!).

I took our old harmonium apart (it was war-damaged as it stood under the window) and used the wood, some to make a cupboard in the kitchen, the rest I chopped up as firewood.

19 January

Snow! I visited Woolworths and bought paint and when Kitty La Haise came in with her child for lunch with Mum,

I escaped to the kitchen and painted the door panels cream and the rest brown. It had not all been grained before since the time it was built (1870). [*Kitty Giblin, at no. 17 had married a French-Canadian soldier.*]

Saturday, 20 January

It snowed and was a bad day for local rocket explosions. I started re-reading Scott's *Ivanhoe* and wore uniform in case I was killed as a civilian. I also re-gilded some picture frames.

Sunday, 21 January

Russian troops seemed sure to reach the borders of Germany soon. (Our Arctic convoys had taken them thousands of Canadian lorries in which they advanced.)

22 January

I left Paddington at 23:30 for Chacewater Halt with a flask of rum that Dad had given me. In camp two and a half hours late at 12:30, told off, so I was cheesed, did my daily inspections on the aircraft and off to bed.

23 January

More typhus jabs and later a walk up the valley to St Agnes. My old lady was pleased to see me. The weather was snowy and a snag on an Anson 11.43, gave me problems, a hefty thump not sufficing. A new Signals Workshop truck had to be fitted out, but this was OK. Helped out by secret swigs at my rum flask. This was stolen shortly after.

27 January

In a gale with sleet I explored the rocks and caves beneath the airfield, so inspiring.

Sunday, 28 January

I went to the Toc H., Bolingley, and purchased chocolate and Brylcreem. We then commenced a regime of frying eggs and making tea illegally in the hut, almost daily. We had arms inspection and temporarily handed in the ammunition. I recommenced sending Mother my laundry. I had an unsuccessful egg hunt so Mother had to make do with £1 and buy her own birthday present from me.

[*The war damage index at Lewisham Central Library records further slight damage to 21 St Norbert Rd on 2 February.*]

5 February

I got up very early and went for a lone walk along the cliff edge and felt all would be well eventually.

Mother sent six oranges back inside the laundry, so I had extra friends. I went to the St Agnes cottage for supper several times a week.

6 February

Bert Perry and I went off to visit Truro, by train and visited cathedral, good meals, film afternoon — *Nell Gwyn* (second time), beer in evening. Bert is a signals corporal some years older than I.

I started lone walks over the rocks to St Agnes when the tide was right, for my musical and supper evenings. A liberty bus service to Truro was started and I used that a lot seeing such films as *Christmas Holiday*, *21 Days* (Leslie Howard, Laurence Olivier and Vivienne Leigh), *Turnabout* and *Housekeeper's Daughter*. The weather continued snowy alternating with gales.

Sunday, 11 February

I received a letter from Mother about a rocket on Finland Road with our front door and window frames blasted in again and Dad very quiet and sad. I applied for leave but was told we were awaiting embarkation. We had arms parades inspections of our fitted vans. Cinema in evenings and beer and I was allowed a whole day off in Redruth and Truro, but no leave.

ARP wardens in Deptford with trailer pump. (courtesy of Lewisham Heritage, Lewisham Council).

Sunday, 18 February

There was 100% church parade (I wonder why). There was a private, probably unlicensed pirate bus and I went on this to Truro some afternoons without a pass. On one visit I bought a book on Charles Lamb and went to the cinema to see *Gone with the Wind* which starred, Clark Gable and Vivienne Leigh.

24 February

Phil Knox agreed to scramble over rocks with me to St Agnes, then up the valley before the village and down last bit. Film awful *Escape to Paradise*, I did not take him to supper in the cottage. I worked on equipment in the van on Sunday.

26 February

I had a day pass so I went to Falmouth alone, by train and bus, interesting place, a bit closed up. Back to Truro then liberty bus to the airfield.

27 February

Dentistry, then spent the afternoon lounging on St Agnes beach with Stan Walker. We are cheesed at not being back in Europe, it's supposed to be a bloody FORWARD staging post. More oranges arrived from Mother.

3 March

To Newquay alone for the day, without a pass. 11:05 bus from Perranporth. Lovely day stayed until 19:40 train, met nice sailor girl, nice food.

6 March

Camp cinema *Yellow Canary*, could see Anna Neagle, but could not hear for rain on iron roof.

7 March

Decamped with Bob Fielder to St Ives via Truro bus. Lunch Truro, tea St Ives, hitched to Penzance on farm wagon, cinema, *Murder in Thornton Square*, fish supper, then booked bed and breakfast at a house in Bedford Road.

[*Later John noted that this was the day that the Americans came upon Remagen Railway Bridge intact and crossed the Rhine in strength.*]

8 March

I bought Mother a brooch and posted a view, got back unobserved in workshop during morning.

9 March

I have a new habit of wandering to cliff edge, over wire and reading a little way down, glorious, usually alone.

10 March

Bridgehead over the Rhine goes well, we must be back soon. Poached eggs supper at the cottage, I took Bob, the old lady liked his Canadian accent.

12 March

Vaccinated again, not quite a year since last, told off for not shaving!

21 March

Joe Bagley's commission as an education officer is coming through.

22 March

Took Phil Knox to cottage for egg supper.

23 March

Decamped to Newquay alone, 10:40 to Perranporth, 11:05 to Newquay. Sunny with strong wind. Bought Ida a brooch and sent her a birthday card. Saw film *Mr Emmanuel* from Louis Golding's novel. Did not meet up with 'sailor girl' so back the same evening. Parcel of oranges came from Mother.

24 March

More jabs, anti-tetanus, TAB and anti-typhus all at once, AGAIN (don't they keep records?) Arm very sore. Air letter from Jimmy in India and one from Ida. Wet. In evening to Truro flicks, saw *Lady in the Dark*, not bad.

25 March

Kit inspection, we really must be about to go. Went to St Agnes over the rocks in the afternoon with Phil and Bert, poached egg supper in usual place.

26 March

Lovely day. Went to St Agnes in afternoon alone, long walk round headland there then egg tea. I offered money (first time for ages, again she was offended, but soon smiled, said "Take care, SON, you will be off again soon").

27 March

To Perranporth with Phil after the daily inspection of Ansons. Saw *Adam Had Four Sons* good, at cinema HAD ICE-CREAM.

30 March

Have been in BLOODY AIR FORCE THREE YEARS NOW, WHAT IN HELL AM I DOING? To St. Agnes alone, very down, bought 25th Wedding Anniversary presents: Amethyst brooch for Mother, and silver cuff links for Dad, shop will pack and post registered.

29 March

The Rhine was finally crossed in great strength at Nijmegen, Remagen, Darmstadt and Frankfurt.

31 March

To Y.M.C.A. Truro and saw *Prisoner of Zenda*. Wet and unpleasant, but now happy, must go soon. On to Newquay for last look, straight back as pissing wet. To Perranporth, bought book. Phil Knox's birthday, too many beers and gins.

1 April

Next round of anti-typhus jabs. Paid in Belgian franc, (900, instead of £5/2). Postcard view of Newquay to Mother, with message—'Am sorry I can't stay here.'

Ostende, Grimbergen, Vilvordia, Maelsbruck, Everre, Brussels

We drove our trucks through London to Hornchurch, Essex, for night. We were confined to camp. Next, we drove to Tilbury and crossed to Ostende on the *Vienna*, (put out to sea, then waited for nightfall) calm journey, trucks lashed on deck. No food, only tea, drove Ostende to Grimbergen, found a damaged hovel and put down groundsheet and blankets after a meal in billy cans.

21 St Norbert Rd
Brockley

4 April 1945

Dear John,

We were very pleased to receive your letter dated 1 April this morning. The weather has changed and we're getting rain and winds typical of April. I was sorry it rained when you visited Newquay but hope you saw a good film. I am sorry I have not sent a New Statesman this week reason is that I told the warden who usually gets it for me not to do so as Mum had put it on order at Fullers in Endwell Road and it did not come in. I am now waiting to see if she is able to get it this week. If not I will get the warden to get it again for me.

We registered a letter enclosing £4 off to you this morning the other £1 am holding to pay you pay your W.L. assurance. We both have already acknowledged your thoughtful and useful silver wedding present which we think such a lot of and shall treasure very much. Now I must close as I want to catch post.

Hoping that you're keeping well. With all our best wishes and the very best of luck.

Much love from us both.

God bless and keep you,

Dad

Syd's Air Raid Protection badge.

9 April

Drove to Vilvordia. After fixing up some lighting, I went with Phil to a fair.

14 April

Drove on to Maelsbruck (Brussels), airfield once more and was put on servicing a flight of Dakotas all night. Sunday shagged out but in Brussels drinking cognac in the evening.

There followed several days and nights of continuous duty servicing whatever landed, Dakotas, Mosquitos, Lancasters, Spitfires, etc.

[John made a further note from National Archive document]:

On 14 April the major part of the servicing station was despatched to B.58 to re-fuel and re-arm T.A.F. aircraft. This detachment handled a considerable number of aircraft and gained experience of a very wide variety of aircraft types, including jet-propelled. On some occasions complete fighter wings were re-fuelled prior to proceeding on operations.

Unit to assist in the evacuation of liberated Allied prisoners of war. From 19 April to 6 May the unit handled 9,367 liberated prisoners of war.

18 April

I managed an afternoon visit to Brussels and saw some of *A Soldier for Christmas* a play, but had to leave before end as I was driving our party and they had to be rounded up.

3 May

I have been too busy to write diary, driving into Germany, using airstrips prepared by prisoners and Dakotas landed with supplies and took out wounded and ex-prisoners which was a great experience, we treated the Germans with total contempt.

We progressed to Celle and Hamburg. Thereafter, exhausted, back to Brussels which I gradually explored further, small suburban café bars were delighted to see us and the locals joined us and bought us drinks. We provided cigarettes.

The German forces in Denmark and Holland did not finally surrender, although cut-off, until 4 May.

Sunday, 6 May

Day off and went to Brussels with Corporal Maskell on a tram and introduced him to Cathedral, Porte De Hal, Congress Column etc., then to cinema to see *Mask of Demetrios*, and in evening to an American Forces Vaudeville show at the A.B.C. Theatre. Very good, back by midnight.

Germans withdrawing, May 1945.

7 May

We drove back to Everre Airfield, parked our vehicles and went into the city where there was dancing and singing in the streets, tomorrow to be Victory Day in Europe! Treated incessantly to booze, back on midnight liberty bus as I was really on duty.

V.E. Day, 8 May

There were anti-royalist parades by the communists in Brussels, but otherwise all rejoicing, fireworks and guns fired by resistance people. Dancing in streets, girls kissing us, etc. Back 03:00, on duty, several kites to service and a Church Army van drove over to us at dispersal and served English tea and biscuits at 04:00, wonderful Christian men and women, no cussing was heard for a while!

21 St Norbert Rd
Brockley
10 May 1945

My dear John,

I suppose you have now heard the Great News (V.E. Day, victory in Europe) we did both wish you had been with us and we are now looking forward to seeing your dear face in the near future. The people just went mad, and this last two days they have even lit fires in the roadway.

We did not go out Tuesday as we were expecting Jeannie and her son Harry to dinner on the Wednesday and then we were all going out together. We had a disappointment that they did not come I had bought a lot of extra things. I think that something must be wrong do hope it is not her other son. I have written to her.

I had to leave this this afternoon as Jeannie and her son Harry turned up about 15:00. Dad was mending the Morrison a spring had broken but we soon got it straight again. It was just a flying visit they had tea and got away again just after 18:00.

The reason why they did not come Wednesday they were celebrating Harry's return and the Victory. Nice work, eh?

By the way, this morning I had a small parcel from Winston Condor's mother. It consisted of 2 lb tins of marmalade, one tin condensed milk and a small tin of cheese spread, very welcome. She lives on the North Island. [Winston Conder was John's second cousin on the Teague side.]

I am pleased to hear that the food is still good and hope it continues so. It was very interesting to read your plans for after the war.

I forgot to tell you that we went to the second house of the Lewisham Hippodrome to a variety bill starring Anne Shelton, was not too bad and made a change on Wednesday evening.

It made me mad when they shut all the post offices up for two days. We got two letters from you today one written on the 4th and the other on the 6th. There is yet another letter from Ida that I am enclosing. What do you think of this masterpiece?

Yes I am a lot better now, the doctor was treating me for shock as the New Cross lot upset me a good deal Dad says I am still nervy and I shall be quite well when I can sleep in my bed again. There is some talk about the workmen starting on the houses soon but we will wait and see.

*When they get on with it I am writing to Mr Crab [**the landlord**] to ask him to see to the kitchen and scullery. The weather has turned a bit cooler for which I am thankful as it is very hot in the Morrison of a night. Well I think that's all for now.*

Our love to you.

God bless you, my dear,

Mum and Dad xxxx

Jeannie said she has written to you.

V.E. Day plus two

I had to drive back to Vilvordia, more of our equipment to be stuffed into our vans and drove to Nijmegen through awful battle areas, rotting cattle, bloated in the canals, stench of death, The German prisoners clearing up all salute us. Slept in the wagon by Rhine at Nijmegen.

Air Raids and RAF Days

R.A.F. servicing wagon at Valkenberg. John on right.

[*John later made a note from the Official War Diary, 12 May: The main party of 18 Staging Post arrived at Valkenburg and settled into adequate barracks.*]

12 May

I drove through Arnhem (What a bloody mess), via Utrecht to the Hague to Valkenburg aan Zee airfield to German brick-built barrack blocks. Airfield caput. Smiling happy Dutch faces, waves and cheers, flowers thrown. Part of Atlantic fortified wall skirts the airfield. Children are starved and spindle legged. Gave all our chocolate and biscuits to them.

Our German prisoners on the airfield outnumber us many times. Bloody funny, they are all armed! If they were not, the Dutch civilians would lynch them. The Dutch shrug at this British barmyness. Why save the bastards?

No entertainment here, The Hague very dead and closed up, so next evening C.O. who has a mistress in Brussels, organised a liberty bus to Brussels! So I went.

Starving Dutch boys.

13 May

I organised prisoners in fitting up a signals workshop in one of their concrete bunkers, their other buildings except the barracks are wrecked. Others organised prisoners in runway repair. Evening to Leiden where whilst wandering Stan and I were threatened by a small crowd, Air Force blue battledress looks too like German.

We're drinking looted German wine, which the Dutch sell us. Issued with clean new battledress and pillowslips and plates. Bloody hell, luxury!

21 St Norbert Rd
Brockley
14 May 1945

Dear John,

We were very pleased to receive your letter dated 10 May which arrived this morning. Glad you were able to have such a good time on V day. Yes I expect that is what they will do exchange goods for food. Mum has written to the Kentish Mercury safely to see if they have a copy of 4 May. We had two copies, one we sent to New Zealand and the other Mrs Gurnet had. Mrs Gurnet said she had written to you when she came to see us last week so expect you will have received it by now. You can be sure I am keeping my eyes open for any jobs that might be going at Deptford Borough Council.

I should guess that you are somewhere in Belgium. There was another payment due for your WTA today. I now have 8/8d in hand. I am writing this at the Post (Warden's Post) thought it was a good chance. Must now close.

With all our best wishes and the very best of luck.

Much love from both of us.

God bless and keep you,

Dad

(John noted from the Official War Diary for 14 May[2]. A very large party of Royal Engineers and Pioneer Corps arrived and commenced work on building the airstrip, which they completed for Dakotas to land on 23 May. They achieved a runway 1180 yards long and filled an eight-foot wide and eight foot deep water-filled ditch in four days.)

21 May

The first aircraft landed at Valkenburg, one radio repair for me. *Kentish Mercury* received showing local damage. A station laundry set up. I fixed new aerial on Flying Control wagon. Leading Aircraftman Board for me. [*Interview process for promotion*] Letters from home where repairs have started once more on windows and doors. We had to install lighting in barrack blocks from a large R.A.F. power plant.

---

2 *The official war diaries are formal documents written by the officer in charge as a record. All held at the National Archives. John used to go back and review what was really going on — as he would have had limited info at the time.*

21 St Norbert Rd
Brockley
22 May 1945

Dear John,

Just a few lines to let you know that we received your letter dated the 16th yesterday morning. Winston arrived yesterday afternoon Whit Monday. Luckily we had not gone out. I have just taken a cup of tea up to him, so I thought I would take the opportunity to write a few lines to you. Mum has just gone out shopping before getting his breakfast.

We are in a proper muddle the bodgers arrived again this morning after leaving us in a fine pickle since Saturday afternoon. Having the bodgers here will keep Mum or I in[doors] or will have to see what Winston would like to do.

I expect I shall be able to manage to go out with him should he like to go to any particular place of interest. Must finish up now. Will give you more news in the next letter. Hoping that you are keeping well.

With all best wishes and the very best of luck.

Much love from us both.

God bless and keep you,

Dad

21 St Norbert Rd
Brockley
24 May 1945

My dear John,

I am sorry to hear that you are not getting our letters. We write every day. We don't let the workmen stop that. I am sitting in the armchair writing this on my knees there are three workmen upstairs in my bedroom. I got my room fairly straight and we slept up there last night, and this morning I found a hefty crack along the wall behind the bed so I showed it to them, they are supposed to have done all that so now they have been about an hour seeing to it.

Dad and Winston are going to take down the Morrison tonight. He has gone up to New Zealand House to see about an overcoat it has turned so cold. I am hoping he will bring me back some honey from their canteen.

He has also written to his home asking them to send me another parcel to include a tin of Bluff Oysters.

He seems a decent chap, not fussy with his food and he does not mind helping Dad move things.

I have got my work cut out getting on with the washing of the floors I seem to have to do them every day. They are getting on with the little room. Didn't I have a job clearing it out!

We went to the Lewisham Hippodrome last night to see Arthur Askey and some very good turns. The first Winston has seen here he says they don't have a Music Hall back home.

He just 'loves' the Italians. He says they are cowards and rotten thieves. They pinched all their stuff.

Dad will answer your letter also which we received this morning on the 21st not bad going. By the way, Kitty had a letter from Ida this morning she told her all about Alvin but Kitty understood why I was quiet about it. She also said she had sent you two pairs of good pyjamas for your birthday so I do hope you will get them safely.

Dad is going to put some money in the post office for you from us. I cannot get out yet but is there anything I can get you?

Winston gave me a fine lot of chocolate and sweets he had sent him. He does not like them prefers drinking beer and smoking so Dad has got a pal.

I believe the men are drinking tea in my bedroom, hope they clear out before Dad comes in. He will be mad.

Well all for now dear. God bless you.

Take care of yourself.

Fondest love,

Mum

Billy goes upstairs with Winston. He likes cats.

25 May

Churchill formed a Conservative government to last until the election. Main part of L.A.C. [*leading aircraftman*] board, 85% on last, very good. Sgt. O'Leary appeared, Irish, good-looking, smooth, most likely dodgy.

26 May

Wet evening went to The Hague to opening of Windmill Club, a quiet café canteen run by a Dutch youth organisation for us. I had an interesting talk with the man in charge, Christian motivated, promised to introduce me to a Dutch family. Letter from Guy now overseas (he will hate that).

Sunday, 27 May

Up early to see the 'master race' from Hitler's Atlantic Wall leave, walking back to Germany with some horse-drawn carts, rifles, but I suspect no ammunition, a handful of British Squaddies in charge, photographed them, but we were silent, no jeering.

Crashed spitfire at Valkenberg.

21 St Norbert Rd
Brockley
27 May 1945

My dear son,

We shall be thinking of you on the 28th and hoping your next birthday will be at home with us. Do you want a book?

Winston is a very homely sort of bloke aged 30 and he and Dad get on OK. He's a bit shorter than yourself. The workmen have not been near us for the two days and Winston is going to pay a round a visits to relations in England and Southend (some are only friends) starting tomorrow Monday.

I am going to see if I can't make them finish. I understand the second aid repairs, such as whitewashing and distemper will come much later and will be done perhaps by the landlords.

Winston does not say a lot about the 600-mile march hardships but he just 'loves' the Hun. [Winston had been a prisoner of war for three years in Stalag 8B.]

I told him that girls of a sort were waving their hands to a lorry full of German prisoners going to work on the drainage; he says they would not wave if he was near, he should insult them.

Well dear I am going on Thursday the 30th to give another blood transfusion, my blood is used for haemorrhage, for merchant seamen and others. I have to go to the Seamens' Hospital Greenwich in the morning, so I feel I am being of some use in this lousy war. Now don't you worry I shall be all right.

God bless you, dear.

Fondest love,

Mum xxxx

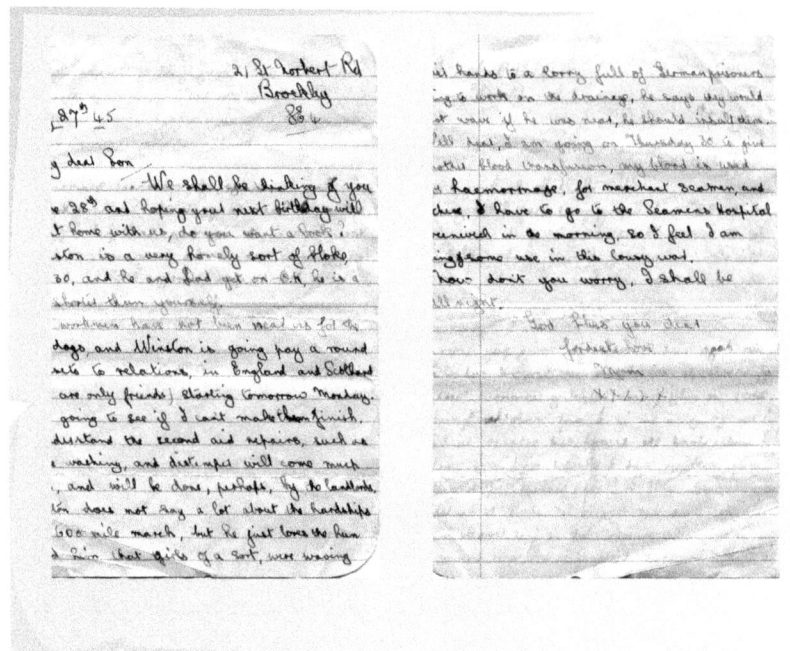

28 May

My birthday, on duty, sick several times, so spent more time in my signals servicing van. On seaward side of airfield a Dutchman called me over to sell me a five-valve Emerson pre-war American radio set, 120 volt AC, Bakelite, for 720 cigarettes. Wet.

*The boys of 18th Staging Post in May 1945:
Taffy Evans, Bob Fielder, John, Bert Perry.*

Churchill

29 May

Wet. My birthday cards arrived. I serviced Oxford aircraft. Set up radio on top of my locker.

> 21 St Norbert Rd
> Brockley
> 29 May 1945
>
> My dear son,
>
> Thank you for the £4 received this morning. I will keep account of it. I had to spend 12 shillings over the usual last week when Winston was here. It went of course in extra food. One item was 5/1 for fish alone. God alone knows how we are going to manage on the shorter rations, such as fat and bacon. What can one do with two ounces of bacon? It will send the house bills up, buying extra fish. The cheapest is 1/6 a 1 lb. We shall all be growing fins. Dad lent me the extra money so I will pay him out of the £4 and put it back when I get my divi [Co-op dividend] in September.

I shall not put the £4 in my book as I think it will interfere with the account but keep it in my spare purse. I cannot, I suppose expect Winston to pay; he has double rations but believe me he had them all back as bacon and fats. He has written home asking them to send me another parcel and he says he can get hold of blankets and towels for me and also soap, these things I cannot buy, so we just have to wait and see.

He, Winston, is mad to think we are going short to feed the Huns, he says let the swines starve. I think he had a rough deal. We only went out once. He does not seem very well and wanted to sleep most the time. He was taken prisoner at El Alamein (I know this is not spelt right) and the Italians were cruel to them. Then the Huns took over and made them march the 600 miles ending at Munich. He made a great fuss of Bill and the others and old Bill has followed him about.

> Dad is rather ratty, these lazy workmen are getting on our nerves they have taken an hour just putting the fanlight over the front door. Well I must go fishing. How did you spend your birthday? Our thoughts were with you.
>
> God bless you, dear.
>
> Fondest love,
>
> Mum and Dad

5 June

Handed in arms and ammunition. Was awarded my first good conduct badge!

7 June

Bob, Stan and I found a way through wire (*achtung minen!*) to the shore (it was called Katwijk aan Zee). With Canadian bravado, Bob stripped naked and bathed and came out blue.

8 June

I visited the Dutch family in the Hague and took the nice daughter to a cinema and then a dance in the evening. Took them cake, chocolate and cigarettes, awful ersatz coffee again.

13 June

I had a letter from Mother saying that Dad was not very well, no details, worrying as he is 67. The next day I was awarded leading aircraftman pay back from 1 June.

21 St Norbert Rd
Brockley
14 June 1945

My dear John,

I received the £3 safely and will take care of it. I will get your book in the morning and send it off with good conduct stripes if Winston thinks to get them. He is rather absent minded, he's leaving here on Sunday the 17th to go back to Margate. I think he likes being here and I do the best I can in the ways of eats, it is a job and things are not getting any easier for us.

Jeannie and her son Toogie came here yesterday she is a good as a tonic to Dad she brings him out of himself. Toogie is very much like Jeannie and he is going to look for you when he goes back, he seems very surprised at the damage we have had. He has seen your photo.

I went to claim damages this morning they could not allow me any more for curtains, new order out, but I got £5/10 allowed for my black dress and damage done to them. As I had still got the pink dockets from the last claim I brought 11 yards of twill curtain with a cream background and a very pretty flower and green leaf on it. There is enough for curtains for the kitchen and your bedroom. It was 5/11d a yard and cost me £3/5/1 so I shall not have a lot left but will get a new dress through Waites and give him the seven coupons and get a bill in case they want to see it.

We have got a few raspberries and a lot of young shoots so we shall get a better show next year. Mrs Giblin gave us the plants last autumn. The loganberries are not ripe yet. Peas and beans are a failure we have had such cold winds. Well Dad is waiting for his tea. He seems better again now any chance of you being out of the air force by the end of the year?

> Thanks, dear, for the '4711' [perfume] you are a thoughtful son.
>
> God bless you.
>
> Fondest love,
>
> Mum and Dad

15 June

In Leiden, I found the university and wandered among the fine old buildings, and found the students' club where I was asked to a concert of modern Russian music. Did not stay to end as girl student told me (perfect English) there was a gala on the canals. Flower-decked boats, Bols (gin), cuddles. I am reading Andre Maurois' *Disraeli*, bought in a Leiden bookshop.

18 June

To Den Haag with Bob, who introduced me to haggling and I bought a German camera for 120 cigs, instead of 600 asked. The next few days were very busy with flights of Dakotas with Red Cross supplies. Some radio faults, some bumpy landings here.

Carrying Sten guns in The Hague, May 1945: Bob Fielder, Stan Walker and John.

Sunday, 24 June

Had to leave van for use on airfield, started walking to Den Haag, lift in SHAEF Jeep, sprogg officer driver here two days. I wandered around and slept on grass in shade. The next day I sun-bathed on duty and had letters from Jeannie and Dad's cousin Winston Condor (in the New Zealand Infantry Brigade). He has been in hospital in Margate, a wounded ex-prisoner having flown back and touched down at Eindhoven whilst I was there! He has already had a stay at Brockley in my room.

I began to receive my correspondence course for the Library Association exams (classification) at Valkenburg.

Plenty of aircraft to service. We began to be able to get hot showers on site.

29 June

Liberty runs were started to Leiden as The Hague such a dead dump. Went with Bob on to cinema saw *Sgt York*.

30 June

To a dance in Naafi with invited local girls as well as our few medical W.A.A.F.s and British nurses from a military hospital. Danced with breasty strangers, got very pissed on cheap American bottled beer!

Hardly slept, up 15:45 drove to Brussels via Nijmegen and Arnhem which is still awful. Got 72-hour pass, I've earned it.

I stayed at the Malcolm Club (set up by a wealthy Scots couple in memory of their dead airman son Malcolm), one night. Next night at Le Grand Hotel, Anspach Blvd. My own bathroom! Treated like a lord, sheets on the bed! Afternoon, to ENSA cinema to see Bob Hope in *The Princess and the Pirate*, in evening to theatre to see Anna Neagle in a play *French Without Tears*, excellent. Then beers in a low dive (brothel), interesting just to observe, back to hotel to bed 00:30.

3 July

Saw all the sights of Brussels once again, then evening, tired, to live all-Canadian show straight from London Hippodrome, *Meet the Navy*. Then cognacs until 01:00. Up at 09:45, breakfast. Had first ever shave done for me! Then I drove back to Valkenburg, when a bad cold came on.

5 July

I did the postal ballot and VOTED LABOUR! as we all are, poor old Churchill! Next day I had to sell a watch that I had bought some time back for 150 cigs, for £2. The food on camp is worse than ever.

8 July

Bob and I walked the correct way to the shore via Katwijk village. He bathed nude, afternoon and evening and turned blue again. After that quite a few locals appeared asking for cigarettes and chocolate. Next day I was covered in mosquito bites. Bob shortly met a Canadian from his hometown and came back with a whole bottle of whisky. He and I shared it ALL IN ONE EVENING — Slightly stinko!

9 July

Somewhat ill but carried out duties, then a Feast Day celebration with processions in Leiden, much gaiety and drink.

Sgt. O'Leary, whom I now just call Paddy, is charming to me, but he is dodgy. He flogs Air Force property the stupid bugger, particularly as he a regular. He is very close about his background.

An old Anson was delivered and I set up the frequencies on a TR1154 in it. Air tested.

14 July

To Leiden on liberty run, another 'feast' and processions. News cinema with a girl. Next day I was duty mechanic, time spent reading, then cool shower, I bet the Krauts had them hot.

18 July

We set up a station dance in a large hall in the zoo in The Hague. Paid for and took a bottle of whisky and a bottle of Champagne, had a good time dancing and took a nice girl to her house. In camp 05:30, but I slammed the van into a concrete defence bollard near my barrack block. Went to bed until afternoon, then hammered out the dent and Bob camouflaged the result with aircraft dope. Then I bought things from the Salvation Army van for gifts home (German artificial silk stockings for Mother.) Dutch Salvationists are running this van.

I complained to the duty officer about food, it did not go down well. Paddy took the van to other side of airfield to service a plane and later asked about the dent. I said he must have done it: he had a sense of humour and said that I was a bloody English shit—he didn't do it as he couldn't drive! I would not admit to it and heard no more about it.

The next day Bob got a whole can of green dope and we covered it all except the brown bits.

26 July

Election result, clear Labour victory, (385–160), I won my only bet, 1 guilder.

30 July

To Hague in the evening to ENSA show *Canaries Sometimes Sing*.

21 St Norbert Rd
Brockley
1 August 1945

Dear John,

Your letter dated 29 June has just arrived. Yes we have read, and heard over the radio that the boats have not been able to sail. I am very much more satisfied now we have the Indian carpet down again as we can now keep an eye on it and I want to get the place a little straight as the furniture is all getting spoilt.

That is just what I should like: a small cottage, with enough ground keep me occupied, but as you know I cannot do anything till you are home as it must be within reasonable distance of your work. If I should see or hear of a likely place, I should go and see it. As you know, these places are not very often going and when they are they're snapped up by estate agents to make big profits on. I am pleased to hear that you have written to Ida.

We have just received with your letter, two from New Zealand one from Joyce and one from her mother. They are very excited at the news of Winston's pending arrival and express their thanks for our kindness to him and hope that you will not have to go east. If you do, they all express the wish to see you and that you will be sure of a good welcome.

The weather here is I should say very much the same as you are having. Hope you like the plays on the radio.

As I think I have already told you Mr and Mrs Gurnett are paying us a visit tomorrow, Thursday.

Hoping that you're keeping well and not getting too cheesed with all our best wishes and the very best of luck.

Much love from us both.
God bless and keep you,
Dad

2 August

Duty driver for 8 SUSP, to Schiphol, lots of arrears of servicing over several days.

> 21 St Norbert Rd
> Brockley
> 4 August 1945
>
> Dear John,
>
> Your letter of 1 August enclosing £1 postal order arrived this morning.
>
> The Statesman has been a time getting to you. Yes all the contents of the parcel you sent were OK. I do not know if the small parcel to Ida was registered or not Mum must answer that. What a pity it was the third-rate play you went to at The Hague. I don't wonder that you get cheesed.
>
> Mr and Mrs Gurnett came to see us Thursday and brought along a fine lot of vegetables. They are, as you say, most generous and hospitable. We feel that we must do all we can when they

come to see us. I am sure they feel at home and enjoy the visits.

One thing, we are able to get little things for them which they are unable to get. They went back loaded with half a bottle of rum three bottles of soft drinks, cornflour, custard powder and I gave Mr Gurnett that fob chain of mine which Aunt Em brought from France for me. I shall never use it and Mr Gurnett liked it very much. He will be able to use it instead of wearing his gold chain. You remember it had the four seasons.

Mrs G also fell in love with the clock you and Mum have always wanted to get rid of. What you call the tombstone clock so I am giving it to her. Mr G is going to make a box for it and then take it the next time they come over, she wants to pay for it but I say no. Well I must not tire you any further but thought it would interest you to know that we do appreciate their kindness and do what we can in return.

I am sorry you were not lucky with your leave as you know we are both looking forward to having you home. Yes I'm sorry the Labour Party sang 'The Red Flag' but the Tories started with 'For He's a Jolly Good Fellow' when Churchill came into the House.

It is a pity about the food. The car maintenance should be useful to you later on. Mum has gone to the Rivoli this afternoon to see The Way to the Stars so I am writing this while she's out.

Mum posted both a letter and The Statesman off to this morning. I wrote after another job yesterday Friday it is not much of a job, but if but if I am successful, it will help me from using my savings. It is for a doorkeeper at the old club I used to belong to – Hatcham Liberal Club Queens Road. The money is only £3/3/3 a week for 36 hours evening and weekends. I should stand a very good chance as I was a member for about 20 years. The only thing that might bar me is my age as they state [they want] a man about 50.

But anyway I went along to see an old friend of mine who was chairman of the club for a good many years and he has promised to go along and see the secretary tonight, Saturday, and see what he can do for me so am now waiting reply.

Do not know of any more news this time. Hoping that you are receiving our letters more regularly and that you are keeping well in spite of your miserable food.

With the usual wishes and all the best of luck much love from us both.

God bless and keep you,

Dad

10 August

Off-duty afternoon, warm, on sand dunes alone, reading, fell asleep. A girl called Greta, pronounced 'Schreta', introduced herself and I took her out that evening to the flicks and a café, cuddle.

Sunday, 12 August

Four of our Dakotas took war victim Dutch children for a holiday in Denmark, so glad, but could not go with them. Wrote to Hopkins the carpenter, in England, Hoppy who had made me a case on our first trip to Europe. Wrote to Phil Knox. I am acquiring and sending bulbs home as presents bought for cigarettes. Hyacinths, tulips and narcissus. Very wet weather.

13 August

VJ-Day, Japan surrendered.

21 St Norbert Rd
Brockley
15 August 1945

Dear John,

Your letter of 12 August arrived this morning (Peace Day). What a terrible sin that little children should be in such a plight and I am proud to think that you are on such work that will help in getting those poor children properly fed and cared for. Mum and I sat up to hear the good news of Japan's acceptance of the peace terms. It is now for all nations to see that such a war never occurs again. What a chance for the new government, peace coming at the opening of Parliament. I expect we shall listen in to the king's speech at 21:00 this evening.

I should think it was right very interesting working on the naval kites. You say will be getting your decorations soon, so should I, but I do not want decorations. What I need in recognition is light work.

We shall both be looking out for the parcels and shall notify you as soon as we receive them.

Yes the Health Department can make Crabb do the work to the rooms but he would plead he cannot get the labour.

Glad to hear you are still getting fresh potatoes. I see no reason why you should not have had them before. Yes we have had your letter of 4 August and I answered it.

I should have liked you to have sent the dates, with amount of money sent, as it would be more satisfactory, and I could then show Mum how to keep a proper account. Anyway I will make a book up for her. You will not be anything down, that is the reason I should like you to send dates and amounts.

I think I told you in previous letter that I had not heard from the Liberal Club.

We are both glad you are able to get some tomatoes and only wish we were able to send you such things. As you say the B.L.A. chaps on leave are lucky. The old saying 'It's an ill wind that blows no good.'

Mum will be writing to you sometime today; she has been busy queuing up for fish and other things all this morning.

All for now with all our best wishes and the very best of luck. Much love from us both.

God bless and keep you,

Dad

18 August

Saturday, Prince Bernhardt of the Netherlands flew in in his little Auster with a fault on his radio. He is quite jovial for a German, I had no trouble with his radio. It was just a fuse, no obvious reason, replaced and tested OK.

The same day I was issued with the France and Germany star and the Defence medal and sewed the ribbons on my tunic. Played chess, sent off another parcel of bulbs to Mother. Letter from home with worrying news that Dad's tummy is giving him pain.

Prince Bernhard in a Messerschmidt with Ginger Eversfield.

21 August

I went to The Hague in the evening to hear Ivy Benson and her band—lively if nothing else. Was told no leave possible. Working here and at Schiphol on daily servicing of aircraft, Dakotas in the main. Weather appallingly wet I am usually soaked.

24 August

Paid my first (unofficial) visit to Amsterdam in my wagon, pelting wet Dutch weather.

25 August

America cut off lease-lend, a sordid act! To The Hague to see film, Laughton in *The Suspect*.

26 August

I worked all day and at night sat quietly in the truck trying to catch looters. Young, one I believe female, hopped over wire where the bloody wagon could not go. They know there is no ammunition in my Sten gun! A lot of bloody good staying awake trying to catch Dutch people at it.

Bloody Paddy can think of something else. To Amsterdam to cinema next night, nearly caught by military police.

31 August

Fifteen Spitfires landed and needed daily inspections; one fault settled OK (bloody great thump). Three parcels of bulbs have reached home safely.

Sunday, 2 September

Told Paddy I must have a whole day off (Bob put me up to it). Went with Bob. Long ramble through Atlantic wall defences to Scheveningen.

6 September

To awful Black American show in Hague ENSA, musical.

10 September

A bad cold and toothache, as usual worked and swigged whisky, also sold German camera to a Dakota pilot based in Lyneham, Wilts, for £3, whilst chatting and repairing his radio. I took a long time to diagnose fault on Typhoon, gave pilot a small bottle of Bols. Posted seventh parcel of bulbs.

Air Raids and RAF Days

We are expecting 90 Spitfires here for a Battle of Britain display. Only 18 arrived today, more bloody work. Drove Paddy to University Hospital in Leiden for treatment. It is obvious that he has caught pox. I parked and found the library and chatted up an ancient staff member, shown treasures. Found I had kept Paddy waiting for me in wagon. He looked terrible. Bob told me P has syphilis and they poke a thing up cock and open it up like umbrella and squirt mercury. A Canadian tale?

Spitfire Mk22 with contra-rotating props, 1944. John is on the right

Sunday, 23 September

Got rather wet inside and out. Farewell booze-up for Bob at Canadian leave centre at Noordwijk, nearby.

24 September

A final, final booze-up as Bob leaves on Tuesday for demob in Canada. The airfield unserviceable due to flooding of runway. Gave Bob Ida's address.

27 September

Runway usable. Sold 120 cigarettes for £1, sterling to shady character loitering nearby and told him to bugger off. Ida writes that she sent me a 10 lb food parcel on 18 August. I don't suppose that I will receive it.

Sunday, 30 September

Supposed to be my first day off since August, stayed in studying librarianship, but called out three times for snags, then finally an 11:43 on a Spitfire at Schiphol, Paddy said he couldn't manage it, so I drove over taking the useless sod to show him (he's the bloody sergeant). Soon fixed it, then drove P to Rotterdam and the Hook of Holland to look at ships.

Navy filled us up with petrol on P's worthless signature. Took Paddy to Leiden University Hospital again. They kept him in; the sod said he brought his own blankets, but they were to flog.

Spent rest of day in Leiden chatting to girl students. P in dock some days, so as Bob had left, I ran things with no problem. I started teaching Jones to drive at dusk.

New BOY officer, F.O. Bostock (straight from university?). He blushes when he gives orders. I am educating him to stand up to Paddy (unless P dies of pox). Letters from Phil Knox and Perry. More typhus jabs. Letter from Ida, Alvin wants money, it needs thought.

12 October

Drove to Schiphol to service radio in Junkers 52 (a three-propeller thing) painted as Czech Airlines. Told charming pilot I was not there to service bloody civilian kites, he said he wanted to be a doctor. Letter from Guy, I continued to teach Jones to drive.

16 October

Paddy's back. Ida's parcel arrived. P wants to learn to drive to pass a test instead of crashing about illegally (the bloody fool Jones let slip that I was teaching him).

19 October

Drove to Schiphol for 08:45 servicing of Dakotas, they are fitted with seats! The sods are using us to restart civilian air service. I stole the buggers' ham and chicken sandwiches. One electrical snag took a long time. I did it, as no electrician!

20 October

Next day to Schiphol, again all day on Dakotas, so in evening drove on to Amsterdam, Jones with me, a nuisance as he is shit-scared of getting caught. I applied for leave and BOY told me I was very overdue and he would fix it. We shall see!

23 October

Had medical, for pox, crabs, etc. off to Hook of Holland by 16:00, on troopship, with drunks going for demob (bloody good mind not to come back myself). Rough sea, most of them very sick.

24 October

Home 10:30 Dad looks far from fit but says OK, and so to bed. I am a bloody civilian at heart, slept for hours. Grapes and radio well received. Sorted my books and papers still packed in boxes from time of bombing. Talked endlessly about work I do and hopes for future and about Ida. To bank next day to try to send money for a divorce. Could not be done as Canada is a dollar area. Went to Regal, Old Kent Road with Mum and Dad to see Bette Davis in *The Great Lie*. Started repainting front room finished on Tuesday when both Grandad and Aunt Kate came to tea. They do not understand each other.

31 October

I took Mother shopping in the West End. Next day walked over to Dulwich and Nunhead libraries to talk to faces I know. Dad gave me a bottle of rum to take back. They are worried about how wet I am so often.

5 November

Left home 12:35 train from Brockley, Liverpool Street to Harwich, on *Vienna* to Flushing (Vlissingen), Hook of Holland.

7 November

I was servicing a squadron of Harvards on their way to Norway as a training unit for the Norwegian Air Force. Nice chaps. Thanked BOY for arranging my leave, talked with him about my studies and he said they must set up an E.V.T. room (Educational and Vocational Training to prepare for demobilisation). That's all I'll hear of that! Soaking wet, servicing Ansons and Dakotas.

USAAF Harvard No.284590.

10 November

BOY took me to a room he had got allocated as E.V.T.. Wonderful are the ways of the Lord! It had no light or heat, so I wired the lights that day and used it that evening! Stove too damp to light. Next evening I arrived with paraffin in a can in the van, wood, and paper and blew my eyebrows off and nearly burnt the bloody place down.

Sunday, 11 November

Told BOY I had religious objection to Remembrance Parade. On duty whilst Windle, Jones et al. paraded and then had afternoon off! New corporal arrived to replace Bob. He is assertive and a bloody bind, would not sign chit to replace my burnt battle dress.

16 November

Beastly cold, our Signals Workshop illegal electric cooking ring made out of a coil of wire in a biscuit tin on which we boil water for tea went out with a bang damaging a generator. Corporal forbade its repair. For our safety he said, not bullshit. The next day took Paddy to Leiden University Hospital once more. The stupid Irish sod told a military policeman that the blankets in my van were mine for keeping warm on night duty. Then he sold them in Leiden.

Sunday, 18 November

On guard duty at gate next to Officers' Mess, a bloody drunken orgy going on most of the night, with whores being picked up in Jeeps and driven in. I stopped each vehicle to recognise each officer, not popular but by the rules. Bad weather restricted flying for next few days so I spent time in the E.V.T. room studying for librarianship exams, lighting the fire each time. Then no fire laid, so gathered own wood in bunkers.

26 November

Saw Flying Officer Roberts and collected Bert Perry's savings certificates to post home to him. He is being demobbed. Roberts showed some interest in me so told him about terrible study room and he gave me chit for orderly sergeant to give me the key to the fuel store for wood and coke whenever necessary. Paddy borrowed the wagon and drove off whilst I was servicing a kite. When he came back I made clear would drop him in the shit if he did it again. When he sulked off shouting abuse, 'Teague you're a no-good shit,' I checked the inventory of wagon tools and equipment, OK.

Thick sea mist for about a week, no flying, did lots of study E.V.T. room warm, Windle discovered where I got to and came and sat and read in the warm.

I serviced Officers' Mess radiogram, valves loose lead frayed and intermittent, was given bottles of Guinness.

7 December

The great freeze-up, ice on the inside of windows, wagon would not start, walking, sliding everywhere. Repaired 11:43 in Spitfire that landed in trouble, OK.

10 December

The Air Officer Commanding's personal Dakota, NK 291, landed at Schiphol and Paddy insisted on coming with me to service it. He did it, I signed. I then drove fast back to Valkenberg where the signals officer was waiting to sit with me to invigilate my Library Association Classification exam. Next day, much bull, the A.O.C.'s Dakota lost radio contact on way back to Lyneham, Wilts.

AN ENQUIRY, I had signed [*it off*]. Paddy smitten in case I should state that he serviced it, [*which he did*]. I stuck by full statement of tests carried out and that we did not have a replacement set. Rations were said to be missing also (true). Perhaps I shall get drummed out!

13 December

To Schiphol, snags on Dakotas passing through. Posted more bulbs home. Bought 20 bars of English chocolate from nice girl at rear of NAAFI in Amsterdam to post home and arranged to meet her the next evening.

Back to more enquiries re: NK 291, stood my ground, Paddy positively oozing gratitude, though he could not resist saying after we left the signals officer that I had signed the inspection schedule. S.O. has full confidence in me.

14 December

Wing Commander Pippett bristled his moustaches, listened to all the statements and said 'Good show, Good chaps in my unit.' We heard no more about it. To Leiden in afternoon for Paddy's pox treatment, told him I hoped the bloody thing would drop off.

Sent local Christmas cards home, also to the Gurnetts.

John on the right.

18 December

Unit dance at Dierentuin, Den Haag, 20:00 hours, took the NAAFI girl, lots of Belgian and Dutch Beer and

GIN, got very pissed, sat in van kissing and cuddling and drove her back.

Next day so many on charges for drunken brawls, I drove off early to Schiphol, where a Spit and an Oxford were desperate to get serviced and back to England for Christmas.

Evening decorated sergeants' mess with electric lamps soldering them to cable, covering the connections with rubberised tape. Paddy and co painting them -they worked well. The mess sergeant gave me a bottle of gin.

Christmas Day

A booze-up. Never have I been more drunk, but I sobered up when a Dakota came in to land too fast and ended up in a ditch. Windy, Jones and I and 50 or so others manhandled it out. Undercart can certainly be repaired, Ginger asserts.

30 December

07:45 service check on a Wildcat at Schiphol.

My pay reached 5/6d a day on 12 January 1944 as Wirelss Operator Mechanic 1, then 7/9d a day on 7 January 1945 as L.A.C. W.O.M.

Reading in 1945: *Three Men In New Suits*, J.B. Priestley; *Disraeli*, Andre Maurois; *Palmerston*.

John in cafe in Den Haag in 1945.

View from the café.

1946

Valkenburg, Holland

At Schiphol tuning and servicing our aircraft radios as K.L.M. were buying some to re-develop their civilian airline. There was regular servicing of Dakotas, Ansons etc.

14 January

I left Valkenburg on leave at 04:30 but did not board ship at Vlissingen until 09:00. Harwich at 18:00. Home 18:30. shagged out.

Sunday, 20 January

On leave, 28 Fahrenheit at mid-day, I might as well be in bloody Holland! I am reading Katherine Mansfield *Collected Stories*, bought at Joanne's 15/-.

21 January

Bought David Daiches *Virginia Woolf* at Joanne's at the Marquis. Called on Mr Hahn by appointment to discuss post-war training; he said get back to work and do the study in my leisure time. Bought Mother a pair of shoes for her birthday: 29/1d.

24 January

Took Mother to see *Pink String and Ceiling Wax* at New X; not bad.

25 January

To Somerset House with Mother to get a copy of Ida's marriage certificate for divorce proceedings for his adultery. Then we walked around St Paul's, I was sad at damage, then to ruins of St. Clement Danes; nearby Dr Johnson's statue has an ornament sitting on his head.

In front, Hopkins, Woods, McCartney, John is back right.

26 January

Leave ended. 14:00 from Liverpool Street. Read Maurois *Ariel; the Life of Shelley*, on boat from Harwich to Hook of Holland. Tried to show an Army sergeant how not to be sick but to enjoy journeys by sea. It was not successful.

28 January

Holland as wet as ever; driving regularly Valkenburg to Schiphol to service Dakotas, some civilian with seats in them, stealing some ham sandwiches.

4 February

My blankets stolen between 14:00 and 15:30. Reported to R.A.F. Police at Guard Room. Installing V.H.F. in Anson NK 734.

8 February

Still continuously very wet, the bloody place is only sand, should wash away. Bloody soaked most of time, aircraft will keep coming in, here and at Schiphol. Laundry back from home, with cake, etc.

11 February

Flooding, perhaps we will have to move to Germany.

12 February

At last, some letters (6), five from home and one from Guy. Nipped off to The Hague and saw *Blood on the Sun*, not bad.

13 February

A Hurricane landed with a radio fault which took me some time. Unbelievably a stupid electrician in England had connected the accumulator the wrong way round! Then to Wogmeer to retrieve V.H.F. and radar equipment from a crashed fighter-bomber (necessary first to test in working order, it was, so crash other causes). Some blood, do not know if pilot was killed.

Air Raids and RAF Days

Hawker Hurricane Mk.IIc PZ865. The last Hurricane ever built, now a part of the R.A.F. Battle of Britain Memorial Flight, together with two Spitfires over R.A.F. Conningsby, Lincolnshire

16 February

Difficult fault on Spitfire. I was at it until 17:45. The Salvation Army van came across the field with tea and cakes. I could kiss this old Dutch lady. Am bloody soaked to the skin.

Sunday, 17 February

I have an awful sneezy cold. Servicing today at Schiphol.

18 February

Notified that I had passed the Library Association Part One Intermediate Exam. Cold worse so went early to bed with half bottle of whisky.

20 February

First day off this year, Paddy did my duty, but delayed working on an Anson fault saving it for me.

21 February

Howling wet gale but cleared Anson fault.

24 February

Heavy snow.

25 February

Heavy snow. Drove to Schipol dealing with snags on Dakotas until 18:20. Back at Valkenburg, tea and cakes from Salvation Army van.

26 February

No flying. I took day off and went without pass to Hague, saw *Rhapsody in Blue*, typical Hollywood slush; I shall never be romantic again.

27 February

More snow, to Hague with Windle to meet his girlfriend (she is about 35, he is 42 and married and has a partly bald head; he is Yorkshire and slowly ponderous but very friendly). Snow each day.

28 February

Most of unit clearing snow from runway. Not me. I'm duty mechanic all the time now. (Oh Gawd, how long!)

Sunday 3 March

The thaw has begun. I filled in a form to sit the next Library Association examination.

5 March

Snow! V.H.F. snags all day. I wish they would delete this place from their maps or get serviced in England. To Hague in evening *Thunderhead, Son of Flicka*. Ugh!

6 March

Given a day off, so to Hague with Ginger, a very competent engine fitter. Bought Mother a brooch, a Delft pottery windmill and Ida a coin bracelet and saw film *Mr Emmanuel* once again.

10 March

My next correspondence course arrived (cataloguing).

12 March

Tame evening in The Hague saw Hepburn in *Without Love*.

14 March

V.H.F. snags abounded. Then in evening to Den Haag to see *Henry V*.

17 March

It became warm and sunny and I started studying in the van between aircraft work, forbidding the other trades to disturb me, some, I believe think me eccentric. Thus free at night for The Hague. Saw again Deborah Kerr in *Perfect Strangers*, had lots of cognac with Gordon Fairhall (Sandemans).

22 March

Evening in The Hague. Saw *Madonna of the Seven Moons* a good British film. Repaired Stan's radio.

Spitfire mark 22 at Valkenberg

23 March

06:00 to Schiphol, several Dakotas have radio gremlins. Afternoon Valkenburg, Paddy in panic (he's a regular!), C.O. Anson had radio problem, only a fuse. Wet had got in.

C.O.'s waiting to fly to Brussels. I got a courteous thank you. Things are looking up.

25 March

Four V.H.F. sets and five power units U.S. at Schiphol, all Dakotas. What a day for gremlins! One responded to a bloody good thump. One bore Russian markings and a member of crew went in with me. I told him to piss off, but he did not understand.

Evening Den Haag, *Affairs of Susan*, with Ginger Evershed.

29 March

Den Haag in evening *The Stars Look Down*, Cronin novel, OK.

1 April

I am now paid 8/6d a day. The daffodils in the bordering fields are beautiful, a return for the earlier stench of human excreta manuring.

2 April

Made great progress with studies, sent home three parcels of bulbs purchased for English cigarettes on unofficial drive round villages, alone. Evening took Ginger to Sandemans where we both had plenty to spend on cognac. I hope I'm not corrupting the gentle fellow.

Wing Commander Pippett went out of his way to tell me his Anson 'had the very best radio contact under all conditions.' Paddy gave him a smart salute, told me off for not doing same.

6 April

Fine weather continues. A Lancaster at Schiphol with sets so impossibly out of order that I changed them. Bought watch for 125 guilders. Bought Dad a Philips electric razor for 47 guilders. To cinema then Sandemans in evening. Bloody bored.

Sunday, 7 April

More Schiphol servicing and each day to Wednesday. That evening Amsterdam. Saw *A Place of One's Own*. A few drinks, Military Police query about use of signals wagon, I said was on way to Schiphol, so had to drive off in that direction.

13 April

I bought Mother a set of underwear, sort of artificial silk plus stockings for 60 guilders in Den Haag back street. Study progresses in van on dispersal. Cleaned wagon and drove Ginger to Den Haag, saw *Wizard of Oz*, bloody juvenile. Flogging kit is rife, so full bull-shit kit inspection which wasted my study time.

Avro Lancaster No.NX611 'Just Jane' at the East Kirby airfield, the Lincolnshire Aviation Heritage Centre

20 April

I was drunk on site in evening at a demob party. McCartney fighting drunk and I took him on and got knocked down gashing my left temple. He then became maudlin about me as blood poured out. Would I say I fell, undying gratitude etc. Taken to sick bay with towel round head and treated but not stitched. M. gave me bottle of Irish whiskey, I took it.

Put on light duty for two days report form "stumbled in billet". Then next day I charmed a Bedford lorry out of M.T. section and drove friends to Amsterdam, Hilversum, Utrecht, Haarlem, walking a little in each, saw lots of bulb fields. A few more undying friends? Like McCartney? The next day I walked alone along shore to Katwijk.

22 April

Monday morning, very early before reporting for duty, walked with Ginger to Noordwijk and Katwijk along shore. Evening got roaring drunk on the whisky at a unit dance, cavorting about.

24 April

Evening Den Haag with Eric (a newly arrived corporal) silly film then secluded nightclub where we both drank a lot but refused services of resident girls.

John at Valkenberg Airfield, 1946

29–30 April

Stayed in each evening and completed correspondence course lesson two.

1–8 May

Evening, Den Haag film: *Le Bossu*. For next week got on with study in evenings in a quiet room. From time to time others looked in and talked and soon left.

9 May

Camp cinema, *A Canterbury Tale*. Commenced reading Darwin *Voyage of the Beagle*.

11 May

Camp dance; was slightly pissed. Girls, rather rough stuff, collected up.

17 May

Handed over three-quarters of our equipment to a Dutch unit that will take over. Saturday, given an official half day off, so to Leiden alone in van (unofficial) in afternoon. Bought several second-hand books in English near university. Bought two pairs of silk stockings for Mother in exchange for cigarettes. Danced with a girl in a low dive in evening. Drank too much cognac. Drove safely back and boldly up to guard and shouted out that I had been at Schiphol all day servicing kites.

20 May

Lesson three of correspondence course returned, OK.

22 May

Evening to Den Haag to see *La Cage au Rossignols*, excellent.

25 May

To Schiphol to remove V.H.F. and radar from Wellington bomber. Evening showed Eric (quiet corporal) some of my haunts in The Hague. Drank much cognac. Expected Sunday off, but another Wimpey landed at Schiphol and the C.O. wanted the equipment removed at once. After this I drove back via Leiden to entertain myself.

27 May

Gloom.

28th May

My 24th birthday. GLOOM.

1 June

I bought a Browning pistol from a shady character for 80 guilders. I posted a parcel home containing six spirit glasses and a set of wooden eggcups.

Hamburg

The next few days were taken up tooling around in the signals van all over the place. We had handed everything over to the Dutch, even the vehicles, but mine was not on their inventory and I was not posted anywhere. I drove to Rotterdam, Utrecht and Deventer. Then I was posted to Fuhlsbüttel, Hamburg, so having no orders to the contrary I drove to Hanover and arrived at nightfall at a transit camp, Orgdorf.

6 June

When I arrived at Fuhlsbüttel, I was not expected and so was billeted in a hangar with assorted aircraft, including a Heinkel, which I had a good look at. It was made of corrugated aluminium. The next day nobody wanted to know. They did not know what to do with the truck as it was not on their inventory and they had no knowledge of my posting to them.

I went into Hamburg on the electric train to the cinema and saw *Saratoga Trunk*. The damage similar to London, except not cleared up and sweet stench of dead bodies in wreckage.

Hamburg in ruins June 1946.

7 June

I asked the C.O. for leave and got a rail pass to Cuxhaven and the next day sailed on a 'liberty' ship, the *Empire Rapier* to Hull, which I reached by 16:00.

9 June

17:55 to Kings Cross, arriving at 22:45. Home by 23:30, Mother and Father amazed and so to bed.

10 June

I took my uniform to the cleaners and wore civilian clothes.

11 June

I wired a power point for an electric iron that I had acquired in Holland for cigarettes, Mother not keen. Then to Peckham and New Cross shopping and New Cross Empire for a variety show.

12 June

I took Mother to the Tower of London, etc. home 19:00.

13 June

I registered a powder compact off to Ida and bought paper dados for bedrooms which are now only distempered after war damage. To Regal Old Kent Road on my own *Zeigfeld Follies* (no stray girls).

14 June

By coach to Folkestone with Mother and Father, sunny and dull alternately. Dad not too well, I think.

15 June

Very wet. Lewisham shops with Mother, then Gaumont *Gilda*.

Sunday, 16 June

Our church being bombed. Could not bother going to Methodist's at Nunhead, so put up paper borders in bedrooms, visited Grandad, played crib.

17 June

To National Gallery with parents then on to Coliseum, saw Vic Oliver in *The Night and the Music*, not too bad, not too good, home by 22:30.

18 June

We all went to Westminster intending to go on the river to Kew. Pouring wet so to Tivoli in the Strand, Bergman in *Spellbound*. I am very poor company, am so depressed, everyone else a civilian by now.

19 June

With Mum to Regal in Old Kent Road to see *Mildred Pierce*.

20–30 June

15:30 Kings Cross. Sailed 23:00 from Hull, but only down river, off next morning, windy, calm. Cuxhaven mid-day, Saturday 22, No transport waiting, so walked along beach. Rebellious 'I don't give a monkey.' Film in evening, after bumped into one of our officers who said I should have left on a wagon in the afternoon. Instead, off with the officers in Jeep next morning.

Fuhlsbüttel by 12:30, where all remainder of 18 Staging Post had by then arrived, lovely day, evening paddling canoe on Elbe with Dicky. Was duty mechanic most days, evenings in Blankenese or Hamburg, from which a surface underground service reached near the barracks. Saw a circus one evening, *The Wicked Lady* (once more) on another.

Then, I was taken off ordinary duties and set to ferrying three-ton service trucks to an assembly point in a cleared area of the docks. It developed into me bringing back the drivers in a three-ton Austin wagon, so now I have two trucks.

1 July

I was taken off this duty (but still had the second truck on dispersal!) given yet more typhus jabs. I think the buggers are trying to give it to me. Arm sore so went paddling on Elbe and in evening. Saw Laughton in *Captain Kidd*.

2 July

Off in afternoon to Hamburg to see cabaret in Crusader Club, then in launch up river. Visited devastated docks etc.

3 July

Brewster's Millions, bunk.

4 July

ENSA performance of Shaw's *Apple Cart* quite well done.

6 July

Crusader Club.

7 July

Blankenese to Malcolm Club with Dixon, film *Anchors Away*. Back midnight. Pissed. Two good British films *Caravan*, Stewart Granger and *Trojan Brothers*.

10 July

Guard duty REME barracks.

13 July

Hot and sunny. Blankenese in Austin three-tonner (less conspicuous than signals wagon). After midnight I found a dead drunk Army sergeant lying beside road. Dixon and I picked him up, took him to the airfield and put him to bed.

14 July

Up early got M.T. sergeant to take our drunk to his unit — he slipped in — Irish.

15 July

ENSA play *Ghost Train* in Hamburg, well done.

17 July

Boating on Elbe with Dennis, who knocked my spectacles off into the water swinging his paddle. Fairly near bank. He stripped off and as I leaned one way he went over the other side. Luckily we found them, filthy and very cold and used both our shirts to wipe mud off him. In evening good British film, *Night Boat to Dublin*.

22 July

Saw *Rebecca*, again.

23 July

Garrison Theatre in Hamburg London Ballet, excellent, could not get near girls afterwards.

24 July

I was duty mechanic. Dakota snags, pissing wet. Sent Dad a lighter. Films *I know Where I'm Going* and *Mr. Deeds Goes to Town*.

9 August

Giraldo and his band in Hamburg.

11 August

Letter from Mother informing me that Dad is ill and has to have stomach x-ray. I sent back a cheque for £5 made out to Lodge in case she needs money. Duty then 24 hours on 24 hours off.

12 August

A Dakota landed at 21:00 with a snag and I showed my annoyance when immediate attention was required by the pilot, a wing commander. Whilst I was putting snag right, he walked over to the control wagon and instructed the duty officer to put me on a charge for not wearing my cap (improperly dressed) and not saluting him. Ginger Evered always salutes and said serve you right. I managed to get charge sheet lost before it reached C.O.

13 August

To Hamburg, Noel Coward's *Private Lives*.

21 St Norbert Rd
Brockley
13 August 1946

Dear John,

Your letter of 10 August arrived this morning so I thought I must write a few lines to you.

I can well understand counting the weeks to demob. We only wish you were with us now. I hope you're able to do some studying.

If you get posted from Fuhlsbuttel I suppose it is too much to expect that you get posted back to England.

I was pleased you went to see and hear Geraldo and did not think it too bad. We both hope that the weather was better Sunday your day off. It was not too bad here but it still continues unsettled like everything else. Mum and I went to the New Cross Empire last night and saw a very good show called Peekaboo. We both enjoyed it and I really feel better for the change.

> We heard Geraldo on the wireless when he opened at Berlin, and he said then they were visiting Hamburg. All for now. Hoping that you are keeping fit and well.
>
> With all our best wishes and the very best of luck.
>
> Much love from us both.
> God bless and keep you,
> Dad
> Cheer up and don't worry about me.

Celle

14 August

18 Staging Post moved to R.A.F. Celle, XX but I heard that morning that Dad was to have a major operation. Wing-Commander Pippett gave me immediate compassionate leave and got me stuffed into a transport Dakota sitting on the floor, Fuhlsbüttel to Croydon. Home 17:30 then to

Miller's Hospital, Greenwich, where Dad was pleased to see me but was clearly very ill.

Next day was not a visiting day but I was allowed in, in uniform, then Flo and Bill talked their way in, Dad worried at all this, fears the worst. The next day Mother took in eggs bought from Shan and jelly and Dad was pleased when I went in in the evening. The same happened each day.

21 August

I went to see the almoner at Miller's and explained how to get a signal to me in Germany. Eyebrows were raised, 'Seriously ill you know.' That afternoon I went off to Hornchurch by Tube to OLHS for extension of compassionate leave to 31 August then to Deptford Food Office for a temporary ration card. It was warm and close.

To the hospital in evening. Dad lively but said 'Look after your Mother for me.'

I visited each day, the rest of the time doing correspondence course study, the gardening, replacing lamp holders for all the electric lights as some were dangerously frayed with war damage. Then I started painting the woodwork in parents' bedroom. On the Sunday flowers arrived from church and I delivered them.

28 August

Dad was operated on for stomach cancer. I spent that anxious day re-varnishing his bedroom floor and at 18:00, visiting the hospital. I was able to give thanks to God for his survival, but not to see him. My religious faith is still a very real part of my life, though overlaid by my R.A.F. self-sufficient persona. Aunt Kate came and nattered for hours. I saw Dad the next afternoon, propped up, voice very weak. He was concerned at my extended leave and asked me to go back. I saw him each remaining day.

31 August

I left at 18:00. Euston to Hull, and 10:00 the next day sailed on liberty ship *Empire Rapier* to Cuxhaven. Lovely waves. I wish I was a sailor.

2 September

Cuxhaven mid-day. Hitched to Hamburg by 18:30. Found bed at Fuhlsbüttel, but unit had gone to Celle. Next morning to Hamburg, bought a new pen and leather briefcase. So I missed the transport to Celle.

5 September

Celle, unholy bollocking from C.O. (absent without leave), no action. He's a decent sod. Lots of mail. Moved into billet with other signals people. To Celle in evening. 10 or 11 beers alone. Pissed.

6 September

Felt dead, had to hand in Sten gun and ammunition, issued with a rifle and bayonet. Celle cinema in evening.

9 September

Dad home from hospital (I learned later). A friend, Mr Lucas. drove him home in his car.

Daily inspections and servicing on flight, evenings in Celle, R.A.F. Theatre, saw again. *Arms and the Man*, Wyvern Cinema, saw *Captive Heart* a good British film.

11 September

Posted off Library Association correspondence course lesson 8. Acquired and fixed up a radio and speakers in billet (winning friends). I am reading Conrad, *Almayer's Folly*.

14 September

Wyvern Cinema evening to see *The Years Between*, a good British film.

15 September

Dad's wound leaking. Battle of Britain Day. I learned to play bridge.

16 September

Evening to Celle R.A.F. Theatre *The Dog Watches*, funny but no plot. Then too many drinks and got on the wrong truck (135W instead of 35W) and so ended up at R.A.F. Fussberg, 40 miles away. I slept in a guard room cell there stoned.

17 September

06:30 a civilised officer in Charge of Guard told me to 'Bugger off.' Hitched to Celle by 08:30—fresh food supplies Army lorry—slight deviation cost 40 fags.

I reported straight to Flight—nobody believes my story—favouring dirty night out—Oh well! Several nights of study followed.

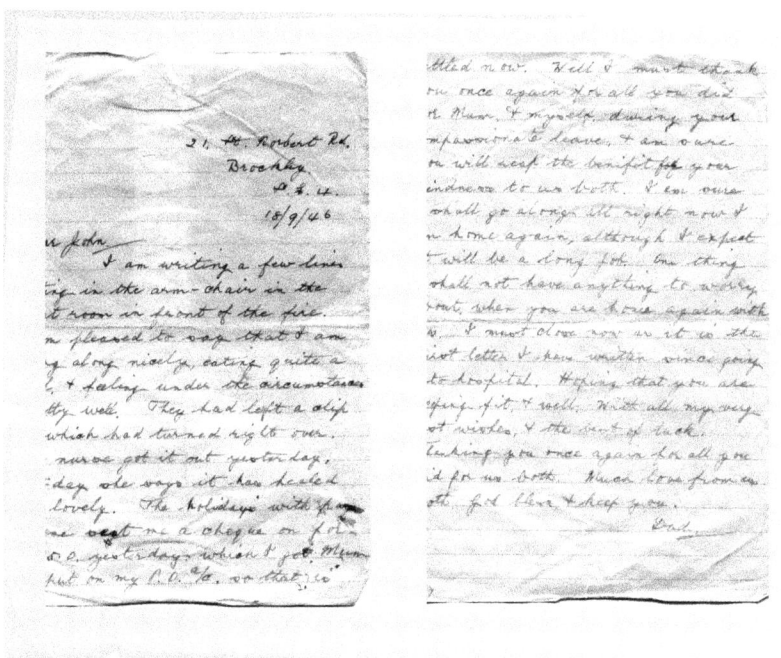

21 St Norbert Rd
Brockley
18 September 1946

Dear John,

I'm writing a few lines sitting in the armchair in the front room in front of the fire. I'm pleased to say that I'm going along nicely eating quite a deal and feeling under the circumstances pretty well. They had left a clip in which had turned right over. The nurse got it out yesterday, and today she says it has healed up lovely. The holidays with pay scheme sent me a cheque on for £1/5 yesterday which I got Mum to put in my post office account so that is settled now.

Well I must thank you once again for all you did for Mum and myself during your compassionate leave and am sure you will reap the benefit for your kindness to us both. I am sure I shall go along alright now I am home again although I expect it will be a long job. One thing, I shall not have anything to worry about when you are home again with us. I must close now as it is the first letter I have written since going into hospital.

Hoping that you are keeping fit and well. With all my very best wishes and the best of luck. Thanking you once again for all you did for us both. Much love from us both.

God bless and keep you.

Dad

20 September

Fixed new volume control on camp Tannoy, having said that it was too blurred to hear. Puppet show on camp in evening, well done if you like that sort of thing. A pointless Kraut effort. Letter from Dad, he does not tell me the truth. Next two nights table tennis and cards.

23 September

I now do 12 hours every third day and eight hours all the rest, unnecessary as not enough aircraft are coming in here.

27 September

Sent Mother £5 to buy Dad a new dressing gown, evening Alan Ladd *Blue Dahlia*, Celle.

28 September

It Depends What You Mean a James Bridie play at Garrison Theatre, Celle. B.A.O.R. [John noted later that B.A.O.R stood for: *British Army of Occupation, Rhine, formerly British Liberation Army of which my Staging Post was a part*] RELEASE PROMULGATION—I should be out in November!

30 September

Celle in evening with three others, lots to drink—then to a degrading strip show. Picked up by Military Police outside, decided to be polite and give all required details pleasantly. They duffed up and detained Paddy M. who was abusive.

21 St Norbert Rd
Brockley
30 September 1946

Dear John,

Your letter of 26 September arrived this morning so am writing a few lines to you. I am going along very nicely and the nurses all say how nice and clean the wounds are and how well they are healing. I have read Jack O' Judgement and I'm now reading The Calendar. There is not a lot in them but they are something to read.

The weather still keeps fine, but yesterday was very dull and miserable. It makes all the difference to me, a little sunshine. I am glad you are enjoying Priestley's articles. We had an air letter from Ida this morning.

I had a lady call on me Saturday, a Miss Headland who lives now in Saint Asaph's Road who was bombed out in Avignon Road. I did all I was able to help her when she was in difficulties and she has not forgotten it. She had heard I had undergone an operation so asked if she might see me. She brought along a new laid egg, biscuits and some rice, and wanted to know if there was anything she could do for me. Anyway I thought how kind and thoughtful she was. She will be calling again and if there is anything she can do for me she will.

All for now. Hoping that you are keeping fit and well with all our best wishes and the very best of luck as always.

Much love from us both.

God bless and keep you,

Dad

[Clare Headland had worked as a clerk and was in her sixties as the 1939 register shows.]

> 21 St Norbert Rd
> Brockley
> 1 October 1946
>
> Dear John,
>
> Your letter of 27 September, enclosing cheque for £5 arrived yesterday afternoon OK and letter of 28 September this morning. Well the weather still keeps good and I feel all the better for it. Only wish I could get out. Yes I always like writing to you and the only reason I did not while I was in hospital was because I was not well enough.
>
> Yes I am eating well and I am now having a varied diet which I enjoy and the doctor and nurses say it will not hurt me unless I feel any effects from it. Then I must cut it out. Of course I must not overdo it as my stomach gets extended.

Well I must thank you very much for your kind thoughts and sending money to buy a dressing gown for my birthday and think it is a most useful present to buy at this time. As I have to go downstairs into the garden (lavatory) straight from bed. I have been using Mum's. Another thing is you will be able to make use of it as well.

Mum has gone over to Lewisham to see if she can get one this afternoon. So I am writing this while she is out. The nurse found a piece of a clip this morning that had been worrying me. The doctor cannot understand how they got below the flesh. He pressed my stomach all over this morning see if I could feel anymore.

No the cats do not come upstairs at all if I can possibly help it as it would not do for them to put their talons into me at this stage. In fact they do not really know me.

I see you were able to get a ticket for the News of the World victory show but sorry you found it second-rate. I hope you're able to see the James Bridie play in Celle and like it. In yesterday's letter I told you I was reading another of Edgar Wallace's books.

I suppose they have to leave the puppies behind when they move on. Anyway they can be good companions. Now to thank you once again for your most generous and thoughtful birthday present. Will let you know what it is like as soon as possible. All for now. Hoping that you are still keeping well with all our best wishes and the very best of luck.

Much love from us both, God bless you,

Dad

[*Maud then wrote on the back of the letter when she got in:*]

Dear John,

I have just got back I've been gone just over an hour. Nobody had called. I had to pay £5 in Chiesmans, the Co-op wanted £6/10 for the cheapest. Dad likes it. It's a navy blue background with a broad white line running down with one of navy blue. It has three pockets and has cloth tie up not cord. Went round Woolworths and Marks to try and get some biscuits for Dad, no luck.

We have plenty of tomatoes growing back in the garden now.

All my love, God bless,

Mum

Price ticket enclosed. [*Receipt*]

2 October

Oh what a day! Flying Control Wagon transmitter out of action with planes circling to land. It was a broken H.T. lead—how the hell did that happen? Then a bloody Kraut prisoner tore up our main power supply line with a tractor. He was not hurt; he had been shoving shot-up German planes farther from the runway. I had to renew 100 yards of cable. C.O. soon on scene, pleased I did not wait for electrician—bloody glad we had cable.

21 St Norbert Rd
Brockley
2 October 1946

Dear John,

Your letter of 29 September arrived this morning. The weather still remains good for the time of year. It is rather colder today. Yes it is very sad about the De Havilland but there are bound to be disasters at such a speed till they're able to get the machines to perfection.

We received the parcel sent by Ida from Denmark this morning and it is really a parcel worth having bacon, butter, cream, full cream milk and cheese. Mum is writing an air mail right away to thank her and let her know of its safe arrival.

No John the nomination form does not worry me. In fact as I thought I had already explained to you the reason of not doing it right away. As you seem to think it is all right, I shall sign it this afternoon and send away.

The nurses still keep finding the remains of the operation. Today the nurse got a stitch out with the knot complete but otherwise I am progressing nicely.

Well Mum was able to get the dressing gown and it is a very nice one, but far too much money. Anyway it is a lovely present a thing I very much needed under the circumstances. I am wearing it right away and find it a great boon.

We are saving all the contents of Ida's parcel with exception of the bacon till you come home. All for now thanking you once again for the fine birthday gift also for filling in nomination form.

Hoping that you are still keeping fit.
With all our best wishes, and the best of luck.
Much love from us both.
God bless and keep you,
Dad

3 October

More work- three TR143's to service. Evening on the town. The centre looks like Chester. I bought watch, pen and razor to use up my cigarette hoard. (Never smoking I use my ration in this way).

4 October

Reported in Celle for release. It was a mistake. I'll kill Taffy Davies who told me I was listed. Bad head cold, whisky. Had to work in pissing rain. Study evening, more whisky.

7 October

Celle in evening saw Bergman, etc. in table tennis display.

21 St Norbert Rd
Brockley
7 October 1946

Dear John,

I was very pleased to hear that you had received two letters from each of us. Also The New Statesman. I am making good use of the dressing gown. Yes the weather makes all the difference to one's feelings. It still keeps bright and sunny but cold with frosts at night. I am very pleased that I am able to write to you every day.

Yes I appreciate the visits of Miss Headland very much, she is one of the genuine sort you do not come across every day. I have nearly finished Beau Brocade, so that will be three that I have read.

Mum has had her teeth done and they look quite well. She should not worry you about them as I can see to all that now I am home. I am still eating well in fact I think

I sometimes overdo it. Glad you enjoyed the James Bridie play. I see they still keep you busy with all manner of faults but as you say it helps to pass the time. I had a reply from saving certificate department this morning saying nomination has been duly registered and filed.

Aunt Kate just looked in but did not stop as she wanted to get round Geoffrey Road. I do not expect she would have called if she had not wanted to go over to the Co-op. You remember me telling you she got Mum a quarter pound of tea well she thought she had taken too many coupons, trust her.

She wished to be remembered to you and hopes that you will soon be home again. Must stop now as there is all news I can think of. Hoping that you are keeping fit and well with all our best wishes and the very best of luck.

Much love from us both,
God bless and keep you,
Dad

21 St Norbert Rd
Brockley
9 October 1946

Dear John,

Just a few lines to let you know we received your letter of 6 October this morning. It is just six weeks ago today that I had my operation. I'm still going on very nicely and the nurses are very pleased with the way my flesh is healing. They tell me I shall have to be very careful still, take things easy and above all be careful not get a chill. Yes the grapes from Aunt Kate and the visits from Miss Headland have been very welcome. I have had plenty of fruit which I have enjoyed very much. The weather has been very cold these last few days and not so bright. I am very sorry that you are finding it so cold.

Very glad to hear you're still getting on with your studies and that you are finding some interesting articles in **The Observer**. I have now finished reading **Beau Brocade** and have started to read **The Top of the World** by Ethel M. Dell. I am sending a cutting from **The Evening News** which I thought might interest you.

All for now as like you I get stuck for news. Hoping that you are still keeping fit and well and that it will not be long before you are with us again. All our best wishes and the very best of luck.

Much love from us both.

God bless and keep you,

Dad

9 October

Charge came through from Military Police—not wearing a cap on 30 September. Wing Cdr. Pippett found the charge incorrectly worded, should have been 'improperly dressed', charge was dismissed. Gave me pep talk about not blotting my excellent record so near demob.

More systematic study followed for several evenings.

12 October

I attended a Berlin Philharmonic Concert, which was very good.

16 October

To Celle in evening saw HALF of an awful ENSA show—waste of a shilling! Walked out and back to my whisky.

17 October

To Celle to see Arnhem film *Theirs is the Glory*, very moving, as I saw the aftermath.

18 October

We have brick-built barrack billets in the style of the L.C.C. housing estate at the top of St Norbert Road, and W.A.A.F. are being brought out to take over some duties here: catering, driving, office etc. I fitted five blocks with R.A.F. radio sets ready for their arrival. Minimal labouring assistance from clueless young airmen I now have assisting me. Older kraut prisoners were better.

19 October

Dad's nurse is now to reduce calls (had been daily). Dr Sommerville continues to visit him each day.

22 October

I delivered an old Thorneycroft three-ton truck to 43/EP Hamburg docks. Quite a day. Spent evening in Hamburg, bought Mother a pair of stockings for cigarettes. Got picked up by blonde but dumped her at Malcolm Club where she was soon taken up.

24 October

I am now listed for release on 5 November, so I started teaching Peter Keenan and Taffy Davies to drive the signals wagon. To the Malcolm Club in Celle in evening. I saw a good British touring cast in *Quiet Weekend* in Celle.

3 November

Went to symphony concert in Celle in afternoon, then obligatory demob piss-up in evening. No after effects next morning and left Celle at 14:40 hours for Hamburg-Neugraben-Fishbeck PDC. Stayed overnight. Tuesday to Cuxhaven, on boat by 23:00.

6 November

Sea calm, boat slow, some of its joints leak a little, engines interesting. Chucked revolver overboard. Hull 07:30.

7 November

Kirkham, Lancs, two changes of train, PDC damp blankets. I slept on top in clothes, can sleep anywhere and wake up anytime, by now.

8 November

Pub at Freckleton.

9 November

Left PDQ [*Pretty Damn Quick—slang*] as civilian in demob issue suit. 12:42 Preston to Euston, Tube to London Bridge, home 18:00. Dad looked better than I feared.

10 November

Grandad and Mrs Green came and I gave them a celebratory glass of port each. Next day I went to acquire a ration book and renewed the pear switch above Dad's bed.

13 November

Ida has married Bob Irwin in America. Divorce from Alvin cost $360, completed during October. It distresses Dad who is very ill.

Ida and Bob's wedding.

15 November

I took Mum to see Marx Brothers in *A Night in Casablanca*. Neither of us thought it very funny. Dad was unhappy to be left, so that's that.

16 November

Bought *The Living Novel* V. Prichett. Played cards with Dad, very awkward in bed.

18 November

I went to the city in morning to buy Ida a Christmas-cum-wedding present. A canteen of cutlery, EPNS, Sheffield £4/11/2 (Dad paid half), wanted it bought now and posted! Aunt Kate came to tea (she now dresses strangely).

19 November

Very wet. Sorted my books. Went to Rye Lane in afternoon to buy pants. Restless not living out of doors anymore.

20 November

Dad very poorly, quite obviously in pain, he has hung on till my return.

[John later noted: He remained in a lot of pain until his death. He had been a heavy smoker, rolling his own cigarettes using Lambert and Butler's shag and Rizla papers.]

22 November

To Nunhead Library (it is the temporary H.Q. of Camberwell Libraries) to see Hahn. I met Barbara, a tall girl with striking eyes. On to Camberwell Town Hall, saw the town clerk re reinstatement (Hahn said I would need appointment). No problem, will be in library department as soon as leave ends. Back to tell Hahn soon as you like, now smiling.

24 November

Studying. Spring cleaned front room with Mum, cribbage with Dad, gave him my sweet ration, it is about all he wants.

25 November

Pynes, New Cross, bought two shirts £1/6/9, sent Old Boys' Society subscription. Flo and Bill to lunch.

26 November

Sawed logs for Christmas. To Lewisham with Mum to buy her shoes for Christmas, 14/2d.

30 November

My brave father has struggled on to his 68th birthday. Dr Somerville took me aside and told me to come for him if pain 'became altogether unbearable.' He is already on morphia. I shed tears in private.

12 December

Took myself off to Rivoli to see *Magic Bow* Life of Paganini a good film.

13 December

Foggy. Library Association Intermediate Cataloguing Examination, 10:00–13:00 and 14:30–17:30, at Chaucer House. My correspondence course tutor had been Sayers and Philips for classification and Sharp for cataloguing, but studying whilst on active service has been very difficult at times. I passed.

14 December

Reframed and hung once more some of Uncle John's pictures. Sherry in evening, Dad had a little. I renewed chatting up young Mr Friend (some 40 years old) at the Off Licence. Acquired a bottle of rum for Dad for Christmas.

19 December

I fixed up my old, coloured lights. Bought Grandad a pipe for Christmas. Snow.

Christmas

I bought a chicken for 19/4d. Dad was jovial and Grandad and Mrs Green came to lunch on Boxing Day. I walked them home at 23:30. We appeared to have plenty to eat and drink and all enjoyed themselves.

31 December

Grandad came again and sat up to see the New Year in. I walked him home at 01:00.

1947

3 January

I called on the district surveyor about the dangerous war-damaged back wall of the house. It is listed to be part-demolished and restored. I now have £378 in my Post Office Savings account. In an emergency, Dad has the services of a Macmillan nurse who lives in Reservoir Road. I rebuilt the garden trellis that shielded the lavatory from view and re-heeled shoes for Mother.

4 January

I went to Nunhead about restarting on Monday 6th although my demob leave did not expire until 25th. I had effectively been employed by Camberwell since 13 February 1939, having had my R.A.F. pay supplemented by the borough to the level at the time I left civvy street.

6 January

I restarted work and was put on split duties, involving four journeys a day to and from Nunhead. After R.A.F. life in the open, that was no problem. Being a male, I am often sent down to Livesey Library in the Old Kent Road, opposite the gas works, to run the service single-handed in the evenings. It is now a cold, intensely dismal shell of a bombed building with no heating available. Dad very unwell and I play lots of crib with him propped up in his bed.

13 January

A transport strike has been on some time and troops are delivering food.

17 January

Strike over. I was reading Lytton Strachey's *Queen Victoria.*

23 January

I received an R.A.F. gratuity of £65/3/4.

26 January

Snow and icy.

28 January

The coldest day on record, four journeys to and from Nunhead.

February

The snow ended on 9 February and then there followed icy cold weather. There were fuel restrictions in force.

No lighting until 16:00 to save fuel. I was reading C.E. Vulliamy *Ursa Major* on Samuel Johnson.

I bought a new raincoat for £3/10 and gave two of my clothing coupons and 4/3d towards a 21st birthday clothing present to one of the girls. We managed pancakes on the 18th but Dad continued poorly. I saw a fine film of *Great Expectations* and purchased a typewriter (an Oliver) for £7 and started teaching myself to type.

I started going out with a girl called Barbara, who was engaged to a chap who was doing his National Service in the Military Police in Palestine. This was acknowledged to be a short-term arrangement for going out for meals and to the cinema locally and in town.

We saw such films as *Nicholas Nicholby* and *Green for Danger*.

20 February

I became an associate of the Library Association and immediately applied for a correspondence course for Final Part 1. I provided a celebratory party at The Edinburgh Castle and asked Johnnie Hahn for a reference for a professional appointment in Deptford Public Libraries. Camberwell Borough Council awarded me **£15 for the effort.**

The weather remained icy cold and I developed pains in the legs from working in the bombed out shell of Livesey Library which was totally unheated. When the thaw came at last, I had a burst pipe in my bedroom.

March

I gained the appointment of cataloguer in Deptford Public Libraries. When I resigned, Hahn seemed genuinely sorry to lose me. I bought a new pair of shoes for 35/9d and commenced subscribing to *The Times Literary Supplement*.

I sent my first typed letter to Ida with a tablecloth for her birthday (it was 26/-, of which I paid half). I was reading Michal Sadleir, *Forlorn Sunset*. Dad was getting more poorly and spoke of not getting well again, and Grandad sat with him to allow me to take Mother to *The Daily Herald* Modern Homes Exhibition at Dorland Hall.

7 April

Grandad wanted a trip to Blackheath and Greenwich, so I obliged on bank holiday, and I paid for a permanent wave for Mum to cheer her up.

10 April

I provided farewell drinks at The Edinburgh Castle on and was given a calf leather wallet with gold leaf initials.

14 April

I enjoyed my first day at Deptford but the next day was tragic. My poor dear cat Billie was run over on the railway. One back paw hanging by a thread. I was at work and Mother got the Co-op chemist to drug him. How long was he in agony, dragging himself back to die at home? I shall miss my poor dear pet deeply. How sad after surviving all the horrible bombing.

Next, I added a bell to Dad's bedside temporary wiring (electric razor and radio). He is very ill all the time now, in great pain and irritable (of course). I began lunching at Pynes each day.

26 April

I was money-taker at Goldsmiths College for a Deptford Municipal and Civic Arts Concert. I joined the National Book League (10/6d p.a.).

4 May

Babs, as I now called her, told me that her fiancé was coming home for leave, within weeks, so we decided that the only fair and proper thing to do was to stop seeing each other forthwith. She married him.

5 May

Dad had a heart attack

6 May

I was up until 04:40, watching by him, when he died in his sleep. I fixed his eyes and jaw and at 05:00 Mother went to call for the nurse and at 06:00 I telephoned the doctor.

7 May

I registered Dad's death, cabled Ida and wrote her an air letter, put a notice in the *Kentish Mercury*, and arranged a Co-op funeral with an elm coffin with brass fittings for £23/10.

Lots of Dad's friends came to see him on the next day, as is customary and I had the coffin screwed down in the late afternoon.

The funeral was a private service at Forest Hill Cemetery, conducted by the vicar of St Catherine's, Reverend R. Shute, with whom Dad had had much to do as an air-raid warden at the nearby post. It was a fine sunny day and Bill and Flo were present. Kate, Miss Headland, Mrs Green, neighbours and two air-raid warden friends, Bob Tatum and Mrs Ault.

25 May

I took up the upstairs front room carpet and had it collected for cleaning, took up and disposed of the linoleum and scrubbed and painted the floorboards.

28 May

Uncle Bill is not well so we took my remaining store of whisky over to him (two bottles). Clare Headland made me an iced sponge cake for my 25th birthday.

6 June

Mother met me for lunch in Pynes (ham and salad, followed by ice-cream, 3/1d each. I introduced her to Miss De Montmorency, who joined us at lunch several times in succeeding weeks. I started serious study for my finals.

I bought a lampshade and a BIRO PEN with money that Dad had given me to ensure that I had a birthday present from him. Biro pens are a new invention and not reliable. After three weeks I took it back to Pynes for a free replacement as it ran out.

(My diaries up to that point were written in fountain pen and ink then Biro took over!)

10 June

I started refurbishing the furniture after war damage, having the dining room chairs re-upholstered and re-polished for £5 each and replacement glass fitted to the bookcase that I had inherited from Aunt Emm. Everything cost more to repair than the war-damage claim allowed for.

20 June

I think that Mother must have been whingeing in her letters abroad, for a 1.18 1bs food parcel arrived from Ida and on the next day a food parcel arrived from the folk in New Zealand.

30 June

We heard that Uncle Bill had collapsed on the street and was in hospital.

2 July

We visited Uncle Bill as he was in Croydon General Hospital for a week or so and recovered.

4 July

Lots of gardening/allotment activity, planting the late peas and beans and planting the tomatoes in the open.

9 July

I enjoyed a Library Association Annual General Meeting at Cambridge, with arranged visits to colleges, backs[3], etc. I sent 10/6d to my Old Boys War Memorial appeal. My duties are 13:00–19:00, 09:00–19:00, off, 09:00–19:00, 09:00–13:00, and 09:00–19:00. The hours and the Saturday duties had the advantage of allowing the mid-week day off.

13 July

Mother and I enjoyed a lovely hot sunny day on a coach trip to Hastings, with good food. (Prices have gone up). I am studying hard, with many books borrowed by post.

---

3 The 'back's are the green area where the colleges back down to the river.

18 July

I went to Wandsworth to see Bunny Halls in *This Happy Breed*, she is so good! The next day Mother had poor Snoonie put to sleep and we were so sad as she was Dad's favourite cat and the only one to feature in his diary, where he had recorded 'Snoonie born 16 July 1938' (another tough war survivor).

24 July

I went to County Hall to get a civilian driving licence, but I can't buy a car until I can hire a nearby garage. You are not allowed to leave cars on the street all night without lights.

30 July

Mother got her first spectacles (for reading), so I too went to Bakers and purchased smart new ones.

August

Mother and I went up the river from Westminster to Richmond and back, getting home by 22:30. I sent by registered post to Ida five of Uncle John's paintings, which I had inherited. The upstairs landing had never been wired for electric light, so I did that one Saturday evening after working from 09:00–19:00. I collected my suit from my Jewish tailor in Lewisham; it had taken six months and 16 days because everyone needs new clothes.

1 September

I took Mother to Margate for a day's outing by coach, 10:00 from New Cross, a lovely hot sunny day.

7 September

I have picked 8¼ lbs of tomatoes so far.

8 September

A letter from Aunt Flo informed us that Uncle Bill was still alive and kicking and that Fred had married a fortnight previously.

10 September

Mother and I went by coach to Bognor and the following day Aunt Blanche went with Mother to Hastings, so I took the opportunity for a lone day's rambling, to Gravesend, Gads Hill, Cobham and Luddesdown and had two good meals.

12 September

I repainted the stairs in white enamel (the paint cost 10/6d.) A new vacuum cleaner arrived from Barkers of Kensington to replace our ailing pre-war Gamages model.

20 September

Mother purchased a black kitten for 10/- (nine inches long, supposed to take Billy-boy's place). She also planted aconites and crocuses on the family grave. I bought an electric fire for my bedroom, 22/6d, a poplin shirt for £2/7 (a luxury), and a trilby hat 15/6d to replace the demob one.

25 September

I started librarianship classes at Clapham for the finals, going on from work for a class from 20:00–21:30.

October

Arising out of my work, I sold tickets and took the money at musical concerts at Goldsmith's College, New Cross run by the Deptford Arts and Civic Society. Grandad and Mother came to some, (e.g. R.A. Band).

One of Dad's air raid warden, colleagues, Bob Tatum, was an artist and he brought along two of his drawings of Dad and in return we gave him a choice of two of Uncle John's unframed paintings. Then Ida, having received the ones I sent her, wanted more.

30 October

Now well used to shortages in the shops, I bought Clare Headland a table lamp for Christmas at Pynes (£2/10), she comes to tea about once a fortnight, having been a devoted visitor of Dad's when he was ill. Mr and Mrs Meaden, for long resident caretakers of Deptford Central Library, retired and their basement flat is taken over for library use.

The typist is very bad and I have to reject some cards several times.

9 November

The anniversary of Ida's wedding and of my return from war service. I was elected to serve on the Branch NALGO executive committee.

From mid-November to mid-December, I went out with a library girl, Iris Carter, but we were never at all seriously interested in one another.

20 December

I went to a dance at Goldsmith's College and walked Dorothea home and my life was changed.

Wedding of John and Dorothea 9 July 1949.

Afterword

John and Dorothea married in July 1949 and lived upstairs in his mother's house. Their son was born a year later followed by their daughter in 1951. They were able to buy their own house in Bromley in 1954.

John ascended rapidly in the library service being appointed chief cataloguer at Chelsea Public Library, and finishing his career as the chief librarian of City University with a large staff. He studied for, and obtained, a degree in economics by evening class.

He loved his work but decided to retire early at 60 to save two of his staff from being made redundant. He then used his energies on the executive committee of the London Society and the Microfilm Association.

John and Dorothea set up Synjon Books together, sharing their love of history. They published Dorothea's memories as 'A London Life'. Their old age was spent in a village in Kent. Theirs was a happy marriage and during his very long retirement John's greatest joy was spending time with his three grandchildren and three great-grandchildren.

R.A.F. Postings

- Padgate, Blackpool, Lancashire
- Yatesbury, Wiltshire
- Mona, Anglesey
- Cranwell (twice), Lincolnshire
- Pwllheli—Driving School, Wales
- Halfpenny Green (twice), Staffordshire
- Lyneham, Wiltshire
- Then in Europe:
- Everre, Brussels
- Eindhoven, Netherlands
- Diest, Belgium (not an airfield)
- Nivelles, Belgium (not an airfield)

- Perranporth, Cornwall, UK
- Ostende, Belgium
- Grimbergen, Belgium
- Vilvordia, Belgium
- Maelsbruck, Belgium
- Everre, Belgium
- Brussels, Belgium
- Valkenburg, Holland
- Fuhlsbüttel, Hamburg, Germany
- Celle, Germany

www.ingramcontent.com/pod-product-compliance
Lightning Source LLC
Chambersburg PA
CBHW062055290426
44110CB00022B/2600